Annotated Shakespeare
Vol. 31
Sponsored by the Shakespeare Society of China
Chief Editor：Qiu Ke’an（裘克安）

CYMBELINE

With Introduction and Notes

by

Qiu Ke’an
裘 克 安

The Commercial Press
Beijing，2007

内 容 提 要

《辛白林》是莎士比亚晚期创作的传奇剧之一，记不列颠（古英国）国王辛白林、公主伊摩琴和宫廷其他人物以及不列颠和罗马关系的一系列曲折离奇的故事。最后除两个十足的恶人罪有应得死去外，其他的人各自认识到自己的错误，相互宽恕，达到友爱和平的喜剧结果。

威廉·莎士比亚

总　序

莎士比亚研究在新中国有过不平坦的道路和坎坷的命运。解放后不久,大家纷纷学俄语,学英语的人数骤减。研究英国文学,要看苏联人怎么说。“文革”十年,莎士比亚同其他西方“资产阶级”作家一样被打入冷宫。改革开放以后,1978 年人民文学出版社出版了在朱生豪译文基础上修订补足的《莎士比亚全集》。随之又出版了一些个别剧的不同译本,如方平译的《莎士比亚喜剧五种》(1979 年)和卞之琳译的《莎士比亚悲剧四种》(1988 年)。梁实秋的译本,现在大陆上也可以读到了。评介和研究莎士比亚的文章,从“文革”结束后才逐渐多起来。

但是,目前多数人学习、欣赏和研究莎士比亚,是通过中译文来进行的。精通英语而研究莎士比亚的学者不是没有,然而他们人数不多,年纪却老迈了。最近若干年,才有一些年轻人到英国或美国去学习和研究莎士比亚。

1981 年我就想到有必要在中国出版我们自己注释的莎士比亚著作。谈起来,许多朋友都赞成。1984 年中国莎士比亚研究会筹备和成立时,我自告奋勇,联系了一些志同道合的学者,共同开始编写莎士比亚注释本。商务印书馆大力支持出版这套丛书。到 2002 年底已出书 26 种,而且第一次印刷版已全部售完。这证明这套丛书是很受欢迎的。

要知道,莎士比亚是英语文学中最优秀的代表人物,他又是英语语言大师,学习、欣赏和研究他的原著,是译文无法替代的。商务印书馆以她的远见卓识,早在 1910 年和 1921—1935 年间,就出版过几种莎士比亚剧本的注释本,以满足这方面的需求。那时的教会学校学生英文水平高,能读莎著;不但大学生能读,连有些中学生都能读。可从那时以后,整整 50 年中国就没印过原文的莎士比亚。

世界各国,莎著的注释本多得不计其数。如果唯独中国没有,实在说不过去。如果没有,对于中国知识分子欣赏和研究莎士比亚十分不利。近年来,中国人学英语的越来越多了,他们的英语水平也逐渐提高了。因此,也存在着一定的读者市场。

有了注释本,可以为明天的莎士比亚研究提供一个可靠的群众基础。而译本显然不能提供可靠的基础。

莎士比亚是16、17世纪之交的作者,他写的又是诗剧。对于现代的读者,他的英语呈现着不少的困难。不要说掌握了现代英语的中国读者,就是受了一般教育的英、美人士,在初读莎士比亚原著时也面临许多障碍,需要注释的帮助。

莎士比亚的时代,英语正从受屈折变化拘束的中世纪英语,向灵活而丰富的现代英语转变。拉丁语和法语当时对英语影响很大。而莎士比亚对英语的运用又有许多革新和创造。

主要的困难可以归纳为以下几个方面,也就是注释要提供帮助的方面:(一)词汇:许多词虽然拼法和现在一样,但具有不同的早期含义,不能望文生义。另有一些词拼法和现在不一样,而含义却相同。莎士比亚独创了一些词。他特别喜欢用双关语,在他创作的早期尤其如此。而双关语是无从翻译的。这是译本无论如何也代替不了注释本的原因之一。

让我们举《哈姆莱特》剧中,男主角出场后最初讲的几句话为例:

King:But now,my cousin Hamlet,and my son—
Hamlet〔Aside〕:A little more than kin,and less than kind!
King:How is it that the clouds still hang on you?
Hamlet:Not so,my lord. I am too much i' the sun.

●梁实秋的译文如下:

王:现在,我的侄子哈姆雷特,也是我的儿子,——
哈[旁白]:比侄子是亲些,可是还算不得儿子。
王:怎么,你脸上还是罩着一层愁云?
哈:不是的,陛下;我受的阳光太多了。

●卞之琳的译文如下:

王:得,哈姆雷特,我的侄子,我的儿——

哈[旁白]:亲上加亲,越亲越不相亲!

王:你怎么还是让愁云惨雾罩着你?

哈:陛下,太阳大,受不了这个热劲"儿"。

●朱生豪的译文如下:

王:可是来,我的侄儿哈姆莱特,我的孩子——

哈[旁白]:超乎寻常的亲族,漠不相干的路人。

王:为什么愁云依旧笼罩在你的身上?

哈:不,陛下;我已经在太阳里晒得太久了。

这里,主要困难在于莎士比亚让哈姆莱特使用了 kin 和 kind 以及 son 和 sun 两组双关语,kind 一字又有双关意义,翻译无法完全表达,只能各译一个侧面。结果,梁和卞两先生还得用注释补足其义,朱译则连注释也没有。这种地方,能读原文注释本的人才能充分领略莎氏原意。

哈姆莱特在旁白里说:比亲戚多一点——本来我是你的侄子,现在又成了你的儿子,确实不是一般的亲戚关系啊;然而却比 kind 少一点——kind 有两层意思,一是"同类相求"的亲近感,一是"与人为善"的善意感,我同你没有共同语言,我也不知道你是安的什么心。这话只能对自己说,在舞台上假定对方是听不到的。哈姆莱特的第二句话是公开的俏皮话:哪里有什么阴云呀,我在太阳里晒得不行呢。sun 是跟 clouds 相对;太阳又意味着国王的恩宠,"你对我太好了,我怎么会阴郁呢?"sun 又跟 son 谐音,"做你的儿子,我领教得够了。"原文并不是像梁实秋所说的那样晦涩难解。可是含义太复杂,有隐藏的深层感情,所以无法译得完全。

(二)语法。有些现象,按现代英语语法的标准看,似乎是错误的,但在当时并不错,是属于中世纪英语的残余因素。例如有些动词过去分词的词尾变化、代词的所有格形式、主谓语数的不一致、关系代词和介词的用法等方面,都有一些和现在不同的情况。注释里说明了,可以举一反三去理解。

(三)词序的颠倒和穿插。词尾屈折变化较多的中世纪英语本来对词序没有严格的要求。伊丽莎白时代继承了这种习惯。同时，诗的节律和押韵要求对词序作一定的灵活处理。莎士比亚的舞台语言以鲜明、有力、生动为首要考虑，有时他就把语法和句法放在从属的地位。在激动的台词中，由于思路、感情的变化，语言也常有脱出常规的变化。这些地方，有了注释的指点，理解就容易得多。

（四）典故。莎士比亚用典很多。古希腊、罗马神话，《圣经》故事，英国民间传说，历史轶事……他都随手拈来。其中有一大部分对于英、美读者来说乃是常识。但中国读者就很需要注释的帮助。

（五）文化背景。注释可以提供关于基督教义、中世纪传统观点、文艺复兴时期新的主张、英国习俗等方面的知识。

除上述以外，还有莎剧中影射时事，以及版本考据诸问题，在注释本中可以详细论述，也可以简单提及。

世界文豪莫不是语言大师，而要真正理解和欣赏一位大师的文笔，当然非读他的原著不成。出版莎士比亚注释本，首先是为了让中国读者便于买到和读到他的原著。不过我们自知现出的二十几种在版本、注释和其他方面还存在不足之处，希望读者多提意见，以便今后不断改进。

裘克安

前　言

《辛白林》是莎士比亚晚期传奇剧之一，约创作于 1609 年，于《雅典的泰门》之后，《冬天的故事》之前。

所谓传奇剧，英文叫 romance，也可译作“罗曼史”。它的情节带传奇性，从悲剧性的冲突，发展到喜剧性的结局。这种戏莎士比亚写了五部。

辛白林是英国古代国名尚称“不列颠”时期的一个国王，约于公元 5—40 年在位。罗马大将裘力斯·凯撒于公元前 54 年两次入侵不列颠之后，不列颠对罗马负有纳贡的义务。那时基督教还没有传到不列颠，不列吞人（Britons）除本地的原始宗教外，还信奉一些罗马神话。

莎士比亚的《辛白林》不是历史剧，而是用几个传说故事组成的。我们以辛白林国王为中心，介绍剧情的几条线索如下：

（1）辛白林国王昏庸专横，听信谗言，放逐了老臣培拉律斯。培拉律斯为了报复，偷走国王的两个男孩，得到他们的保姆的帮助，一起逃到威尔士山野洞穴匿居。二十年后，两个王子长大了也不知道自己的出身。

（2）辛白林国王的王后去世，他盲目地娶了一个寡妇做继后。这寡妇还带来一个拖油瓶克洛顿。这母子俩一肚子坏水，居心夺取王位。辛白林剩下一个有继承权的女儿伊摩琴。伊摩琴公主有貌有德有智，看不上克洛顿，却爱上了宫中养着的一个贫穷孤儿波塞摩斯（其名字意为遗腹子），并和他秘密结了婚。辛白林大怒，又受继后挑唆，将波塞摩斯放逐，将女儿软禁。

波塞摩斯流亡罗马，偶然在一群意大利男子面前夸耀自己的妻子美貌和忠贞。不怀好意的意大利纨绔子弟阿埃基摩用激将法和他打赌，骗取他的戒指为介绍信物，前往不列颠王宫，试图破坏伊摩琴的贞洁。阿埃基摩引诱伊摩琴遭到严词拒绝，便设计躲在一只木箱内，寄放到伊摩琴的卧房，入夜窃取她的手镯，偷看她身上的记认，默识室内的陈设，回罗马后诡称诱奸已经得手。波塞摩斯信以为真，大为沮丧，不仅输掉赌注，还起意杀死背叛自己的妻子，指示他的老仆去执行。

老仆回到不列颠不忍下手，将真相告知女主人伊摩琴。伊摩琴本欲自尽，为老仆说服，化装成男子，潜出宫外，取道威尔士，前往罗马寻找丈夫。她在山洞和老臣培拉律斯及其带养的两个男青年(其实是她自己的两个哥哥)相遇，受到他们的欢迎和接待，暂住一起。

公主失踪，宫内大乱。克洛顿换上波塞摩斯的衣装，追到威尔士，企图杀死波塞摩斯和强暴伊摩琴，不料与伊摩琴的大哥相遇，发生口角，被大哥砍死，割去头颅，抛入溪流；无头尸则弃之荒野。

伊摩琴在山洞偶感不适，饮了老仆从继后那里带来的药，顿时失去知觉。(此药为继后意在用来毒死几个对手的，但已为医师调换为麻醉剂，饮者形同死去，但过一段时间仍能苏醒。)培拉律斯等三人以为伊摩琴病死，十分伤心，为她唱了挽歌，覆以花草。伊摩琴醒来，发现近处克洛顿的无头尸，误以为是波塞摩斯的尸着，悲痛欲绝。适值罗马使臣和督军路歇斯路过，收其作为侍童，携之而去。

(3) 辛白林国王受继后及其子克洛顿的挑唆，毁弃不列颠对罗马纳贡的成例，开启战端。罗马和平使臣路歇斯去而复来，成为罗马军团的督军。战争不利，辛白林被俘，不列颠危在旦夕。幸而老臣培拉律斯和他培养的两位王子在一条狭巷里英勇抵挡罗马军团，转危为安，反守为攻。随罗马人回到不列颠的波塞摩斯也抱着对杀妻的忏悔心情为祖国效力立功。国王被救出，两军言和。

以上逐臣、逐婿、树敌三件大事都是辛白林国王的错误造成。到剧本最后第五幕第五场时，比辛白林更坏的继后已疯狂而死，其子克洛顿已被杀，两个最坏的人得到报应。其余所有剧中人齐集宫廷，辛白林国王论功行赏，想不到在其间揭露了继后的毒计，揭破了阿埃基摩的恶作剧，辛白林认女，认子，认老臣，认婿，认对罗马纳贡的义务，承认自己的一系列愚蠢，并宣布“宽恕是适用于所有人的箴言”(Pardon's the word to all, V v 422)，包括波塞摩斯对良心发现的阿埃基摩的宽恕。宽恕、赦免、原谅(pardon, spare, forgive)以及罗马和不列颠之间的和平友好就是本剧结束时的主调。

若将《辛白林》和《李尔王》相比，辛白林做的错事比李尔更多、更严重。然而这两位不列颠国王的结局却如此之不同，从李尔的悲剧到辛白林的喜剧性传奇，我们可以看到莎士比亚在创作晚期在思想和情趣方面的巨大变化。

没有变的，是莎士比亚善于运用几个故事素材，将之巧妙编织成为波澜起伏的复杂情节的本领、善于创造人物个性的本领以及善于用形象化的鲜明语言表达不同观点的本领。

说到此剧的故事来源，(1)历史方面，主要是拉斐尔·霍林谢德的《英格兰、苏格兰和爱尔兰编年史》(1578,1587)。不仅不列颠和罗马关系的这一方面，而且“一位老人、两个青年、一条狭巷”的战争场面也是取材于此，不过是将一个抗击丹麦入侵的故事改造成为抗击罗马人侵罢了。(2)后母嫉恨女儿，施用两面派手段和毒药，这来自白雪公主、灰姑娘等极为普及的欧洲童话。我们也记得，莎士比亚在《罗密欧与朱丽叶》中已经用过麻醉药来造成剧情的转折。(3)被冤枉和放逐的大臣，最终还是忠于国王，忠于国家，这样的情节莎士比亚在《李尔王》中已经用过。(4)夸妻子的美貌和贞洁，和人打赌，引起祸水，这在欧洲文学里有悠久的传统。古希腊历史学家希罗多德在他著名的《历史》第一章八至十二节中讲述利迪亚国王向盖吉斯吹嘘妻的美，甚至让他看妻的裸体，导致妻忿而与盖吉斯勾结，杀王篡位。莎士比亚直接取材的则是同时代意大利作家薄迦丘《十日谈》中第二天第九个故事，说的也是丈夫夸妻，与人打赌，吃了大亏。(5)宫中寄养的男青年偷偷和公主结婚，遭到放逐。公主去找丈夫，为山洞隐士救助。这样的故事出现在

1589年出版的佚名作家的剧本《爱情和命运获胜传奇》，可能莎士比亚曾读到并借用。

《辛白林》剧中最突出的人物数德、貌、才三全的公主伊摩琴，她是莎剧中众多女性中最优秀者之一。因此有人认为伊摩琴是本剧主角。如果以她为中心，而不是以辛白林为中心来看待，则本剧写的是一个完全无辜的纯洁少女受尽折磨，最后获昭雪的故事。她受奸诈的后母嫉恨，被凶狠的父亲软禁和咒骂，被愚蠢的克洛顿恶意追求，被外国坏人阿埃基摩构陷，被丈夫严重误解，甚至下令杀害，最后还被他打了一下。如果说“宽恕”，可怜的伊摩琴应该是最有资格讲“宽恕”的，特别是针对父亲和丈夫对她的亏欠。她身边只有老仆、老臣和尚未互认的两个哥哥是对她爱护的。

莎士比亚作为剧作家，对他所创造的人物一般说来处于超然的地位。但我们感觉到，在这部戏里莎士比亚确实是最同情伊摩琴。有评论家认为，伊摩琴看中了波塞摩斯的才貌和教养，毫不在乎他的贫贱，这是背叛了封建的门第观念，反映了莎士比亚的人文主义立场。我同意这是浓重的一笔。但是我们不要忘记，就在这《辛白林》同一剧中，也有不少写到出身高贵的重要性的地方。其次，波塞摩斯其实也是将门之后，他的贫贱只是一时的遭遇，特别是剧本接近结束时，这点更加明显。第五幕第四场波塞摩斯做梦这一大段戏，他的父、母、兄长的灵魂出现，大夸他是 great Sicilius’ (Leonatus’) heir，接着天帝朱庇特下降，宣布波塞摩斯为神所恩宠，劫难将满，幸福在前。还有一段神谕，经预言家解释，波塞摩斯是“雄狮之子”。也有评论家认为做梦一场和预言家释神谕一段，体裁各异，文字粗俗，和剧情的发展没有关系，恐系后加，或非莎士比亚所写。这倒也有可能。特别是天帝朱庇特骑鹰下降一节，是1610年左右起伦敦舞台上一种从天花板方洞中吊下和拉去神怪的新花样，可能是为增加吸引力而增添的。

我们需要经常提醒自己，特别是在读莎士比亚的剧本而不是观看舞台演出的时候，剧中的对话和独白都是莎士比亚为不同角色设计的台词，而不是莎士比亚自己直接发表的意见。因此不足为怪的，《辛白林》中既有不讲门当户对的观点，也有讲究出身门第的观点；既有斥女人为祸水根源的观点，也有称“男人的盟誓是女人的陷阱”的观点。也就是说，在莎士比亚里可以找到人文主义的新观点，也可以找到不少封建迷信的旧观点。例如，培拉律斯有一整套关于“自然”(nature)和本能(instinct)的理论，他认为两个王子身上流着高贵的血液，其天性的火花不可湮没，而且“懦夫生懦夫，卑贱者产生卑贱”，这对应了“龙生龙，凤生凤，耗子生儿打地洞”的说法。

《辛白林》中对古罗马颇多赞扬，包括罗马人的纪律，荣誉感的教育，以及斯多葛派(Stoics)视死如归的精神；反之，对意大利人却很贬鄙，说他们奸恶，因惯用毒药害人而受到咒诅。就像罗马和意大利不是一个国家似的。其实，这是因为莎士比亚对历史时间的混淆，也是英国公众一般的区别性看法，17世纪初的英国人对古罗马是推崇的，而对同时代的意大利人则印象不佳。《辛白林》中有不少夸赞不列颠的爱国主义词句，称不列颠人勇敢无畏，纪律有进步，越来越受世界看重。伊摩琴把不列颠比作世界这本大书里的一页，属于这书，但却没有装订进去，还把它比做“大池塘里的一个天鹅巢”。这两个比喻很有意思，反映了在世界地理大发现时期英国人对自己国家的地位的看法。

英国医生兼占星术家西门·福尔曼有一部叫做《观剧记》的手稿，其中记载他于1611年在寰球剧院观《麦克白》(4月20日)、《冬天的故事》(5月15日)和《辛白林》(日期漏记)。他是同年9月12日渡泰晤士河时落水而死的，这是《辛白林》剧初演的下限。此剧在莎士比亚在世时未曾刊出，首次出版时收在莎士比亚同事海明和康德尔合编的1623年对折本戏剧全集中。

1998年5月12日于北京

CYMBELINE

DRAMATIS PERSONAE.

CYMBELINE, *king of Britain.*

CLOTEN, *son to the Queen by a former husband.*

POSTHUMUS LEONATUS, *a gentleman, husband to Imogen.*

BELARIUS, *a banished lord, disguised under the name of Morgan.*

GUIDERIUS, ARVIRAGUS, } *sons to Cymbeline, disguised under the names of Polydore and Cadwal, supposed sons to Morgan.*

PHILARIO, *friend to Posthumus,* IACHIMO, *friend to Philario,* } *Italians.*

CAIUS LUCIUS, *General of the Roman forces.*

PISANIO, *servant to Posthumus.*

CORNELIUS, *a physician.*

A Roman Captain.

Two British Captains.

A Frenchman, friend to Philario.

Two Lords of Cymbeline's Court.

Two Gentlemen of the same.

Two Gaolers.

Queen, wife to Cymbeline.

IMOGEN, *daughter to Cymbeline by a former queen.*

HELEN, *a lady attending on Imogen.*

Lords, Ladies, Roman Senators, Tribunes, a Soothsayer, a Dutchman, a Spaniard, Musicians, Officers, Captains, Soldiers, Messengers, and other Attendants.

Apparitions.

SCENE: *Britain: Rome.*

Dramatis personae [拉丁]：characters in the play，剧中人物。

Cymbeline ['simbili:n]：传说中的不列颠国王。古罗马人在 55 B. C. —5 世纪初入侵时，把住在今英格兰的凯尔特族人叫做不列吞人 Britons，他们住的地方叫 Britain. 与辛白林相对应，在历史上是有一位叫 Cunobelin 的国王（A. D. 5—40），但剧中情节并无历史根据。

Cloten ['klɔtn]

Posthumus ['pɔstjuməs]：意思是遗腹子。

Leonatus：意思是 lion-born，小狮子。

Iachimo [i'ækiməu]：有的版本作 Jachimo 或 Giacomo，即意大利语中的 James.

Caius Lucius ['kæiəs 'lu:sjəs]：起先是罗马使节，后为罗马征讨军将军。

Imogen ['iməudʒən]：传说中另有名字叫 Innogen，意思是 innocence 清白无瑕。

senators：古罗马元老院议员。

tribunes：古罗马由普通平民选出的护民官。

ACT I

SCENE I

Britain. The garden of Cymbeline's palace.

Enter two Gentlemen.

First Gent. You do not meet a man but frowns: our bloods
No more obey the heavens than our courtiers
Still seem as does the king.

Sec. Gent. But what's the matter?

First Gent. His daughter, and the heir of 's kingdom, whom
He purposed to his wife's sole son—a widow
That late he married—hath referr'd herself
Unto a poor but worthy gentleman: she's wedded;
Her husband banish'd; she imprison'd: all
Is outward sorrow; though I think the king
Be touch'd at very heart.

Sec. Gent. None but the king?

First Gent. He that hath lost her too: so is the queen,
That most desired the match: but not a courtier,
Although they wear their faces to the bent
Of the king's looks, hath a heart that is not
Glad at the thing they scowl at.

Sec. Gent. And why so?

First Gent. He that hath miss'd the princess is a thing
Too bad for bad report: and he that hath her,
I mean, that married her,—alack, good man! —
And therefore banish'd is a creature such

I. i.（表示第一幕第一场，后类推。）（以下黑体数字为行码。）

1 but frowns：who does not frown. **bloods**：dispositions，temper.

2 heavens：heavenly bodies，天体，星辰。旧时认为星辰决定人的命运和性情。

3 does，i. e.，obeys.

5 purposed to：intended for.

6 late：lately. **hath**：has 的另一写法，从英国南部方言读法。**referr'd**：given.

10 very adj. used for emphasis，像 true.

11 He，i. e.，Cloten，the queen's son.

13 they，i. e.，the courtiers.

13—14 to the bent of：in accordance with.

16 He，i. e.，Cloten.

17 Too bad for bad report：worse than can be expressed in words. **he**，i. e.，Posthumus，the poor but worthy gentleman.

18 alack：alas.

19 therefore：on that account.

As, to seek through the regions of the earth
For one his like, there would be something failing
In him that should compare. I do not think
So fair an outward and such stuff within
Endows a man but he.

Sec. Gent. You speak him far.

First Gent. I do extend him, sir, within himself,
Crush him together rather than unfold
His measure duly.

Sec. Gent. What's his name and birth?

First Gent. I cannot delve him to the root: his father
Was call'd Sicilius, who did join his honour
Against the Romans with Cassibelan,
But had his titles by Tenantius, whom
He served with glory and admired success,
So gain'd the sur-addition Leonatus:
And had, besides this gentleman in question,
Two other sons, who in the wars o' the time
Died with their swords in hand; for which their father,
Then old and fond of issue, took such sorrow
That he quit being, and his gentle lady,
Big of this gentleman, our theme, deceased
As he was born. The king he takes the babe
To his protection, calls him Posthumus Leonatus,
Breeds him and makes him of his bed-chamber:
Puts to him all the learnings that his time
Could make him the receiver of; which he took,
As we do air, fast as 'twas minister'd,
And, in's spring became a harvest: lived in court—
Which rare it is to do—most praised, most loved:
A sample to the youngest, to the more mature
A glass that feated them, and to the graver
A child that guided dotards; to his mistress,

21 **his like**：who is his equal. **failing**：lacking.

22 **him that should compare**：the man who should think himself equal.

23 **outward**：external form，exterior. **stuff**：(1) substance；(2) fabric.

24 **Endows**：furnishes，enriches. **he**：him. **speak him far**：go far in praising him.

25 **extend**：extol，praise. **within himself**：within the bounds of his merits.

26—27 **Crush … duly**：squeeze him together (like a piece of fabric ＝stuff) rather than spread him out as it ought to be.

29 **honour**：martial prowess. 下接 with 短语，再接 against 短语。

30 **Cassibelan**：即古不列颠王 Cassivellaunus，是 Cymbeline 的伯父。

31 **Tenantius**：Cymbeline 的父亲。

33 **sur-addition**：additional name.

34 **this gentleman in question**，i. e.，Posthumus.

37 **issue**：offspring，his children.

38 **quit being**：left life，died.

39 **Big of**：pregnant with. **our theme**：subject about whom we speak.

40 **he**，the king 的同位语。

42 **Breeds him**：brings him up. **of his bed-chamber**：one of his personal servants.

43 **Puts to**：imparts to，gives. **time**：age.

45 **fast as**：as fast (soon) as.

48 **sample**：example.

49 **glass**：mirror. **feated them**：fashioned them，constrained them to propriety.

50 **dotards**：men whose intellect is impaired by old age. **to**：as for.

For whom he now is banish'd, her own price
Proclaims how she esteem'd him and his virtue;
By her election may be truly read
What kind of man he is.

Sec. Gent. I honour him
Even out of your report. But, pray you, tell me,
Is she sole child to the king?

First Gent. His only child.
He had two sons,—if this be worth your hearing,
Mark it,—the eldest of them at three years old,
I' the swathing clothes the other, from their nursery
Were stolen, and to this hour no guess in knowledge
Which way they went.

Sec. Gent. How long is this ago?

First Gent. Some twenty years.

Sec. Gent. That a king's children should be so convey'd!
So slackly guarded! and the search so slow,
That could not trace them!

First Gent. Howsoe'er 'tis strange,
Or that the negligence may well be laugh'd at,
Yet is it true, sir.

Sec. Gent. I do well believe you.

First Gent. We must forbear: here comes the gentleman,
The queen and princess. [*Exeunt.*

Enter the Queen, Posthumus and Imogen.

Queen. No, be assured you shall not find me, daughter,
After the slander of most stepmothers,
Evil-eyed unto you: you're my prisoner, but
Your gaoler shall deliver you the keys
That lock up your restraint. For you, Posthumus,
So soon as I can win the offended king,
I will be known your advocate: marry, yet
The fire of rage is in him, and 'twere good

51 **her own price**: (1) her own worth, (2) the price she has paid for him.

53 **election**: choice.

55 **out of**: from hearing.

59 **swathing**: swaddling,襁褓。

60 **no guess in knowledge**: no informed conjecture.

63 **convey'd**: carried away.

68 **forbear**: withdraw.

S. D. (stage direction) **Exeunt** ['eksiʌnt, 拉丁]: exit 之复数,退场。

71 **After the slander**: in accordance with the slanderous repute.

72 **Evil-eyed**: malicious,上接 me.

74 **restraint**: confinement, i. e., prison. **For**: as for.

75 **win**: prevail with by persuasion.

76 **marry**: by the Virgin Mary, a mild oath.

77 **'twere good**: it would be better if.

You lean'd unto his sentence with what patience
Your wisdom may inform you.

Post. Please your highness,
I will from hence to-day.

Queen. You know the peril.
I'll fetch a turn about the garden, pitying
The pangs of barr'd affections, though the king
Hath charged you should not speak together. [*Exit.*

Imo. O
Dissembling courtesy! How fine this tyrant
Can tickle where she wounds! My dearest husband,
I something fear my father's wrath; but nothing—
Always reserved my holy duty—what
His rage can do on me: you must be gone,
And I shall here abide the hourly shot
Of angry eyes, not comforted to live,
But that there is this jewel in the world
That I may see again.

Post. My queen! my mistress!
O lady, weep no more, lest I give cause
To be suspected of more tenderness
Than doth become a man! I will remain
The loyal'st husband that did e'er plight troth:
My residence in Rome at one Philario's,
Who to my father was a friend, to me
Known but by letter: thither write, my queen,
And with mine eyes I'll drink the words you send,
Though ink be made of gall.

Re-enter Queen.

Queen. Be brief, I pray you:
If the king come, I shall incur I know not
How much of his displeasure. [*Aside*] Yet I'll move him

78 lean'd unto: obeyed.

79 inform: instill in.

80 from: go from.

81 fetch: take.

S. D. **Exit**: 下场。

86 something: somewhat.

87 reserved: excepting. **duty**, i. e., (1) duty as a wife; (2) duty of obedience to my father.

88 on: to.

90 not comforted to live: finding no comfort in living.

91 this jewel, i. e., Posthumus.

93 give cause, i. e., weep too and so give cause.

95 become: befit.

96 plight troth: pledge faith (in marriage).

99 but: only.

101 gall: 胆汁。

103 move: incite. **him**, i. e., the king,下行同。

To walk this way: I never do him wrong
But he does buy my injuries, to be friends;
Pays dear for my offences. [*Exit.*

Post. Should we be taking leave
As long a term as yet we have to live,
The loathness to depart would grow. Adieu!

Imo. Nay, stay a little:
Were you but riding forth to air yourself,
Such parting were too petty. Look here, love;
This diamond was my mother's: take it, heart;
But keep it till you woo another wife,
When Imogen is dead.

Post. How, how! another?
You gentle gods, give me but this I have,
And sear up my embracements from a next
With bonds of death! [*Putting on the ring.*] Remain, remain thou here
While sense can keep it on! And, sweetest, fairest,
As I my poor self did exchange for you
To your so infinite loss, so in our trifles
I still win of you: for my sake wear this;
It is a manacle of love; I'll place it
Upon this fairest prisoner.
[*Putting a bracelet on her arm.*

Imo. O the gods!
When shall we see again?

Enter Cymbeline and Lords.

Post. Alack, the king!

Cym. Thou basest thing, avoid! hence, from my sight!
If after this command thou fraught the court
With thy unworthiness, thou diest: away!
Thou'rt poison to my blood.

105 **buy … friends**: pay for my injuries, as if they were benefits.

107 **As long a term**: for as long a time.

108 **loathness**: unwillingness.

110 **air yourself**: take fresh air.

111 **petty**: trifling, casual.

112 **heart**: sweetheart.

115 **this**, i. e., this wife.

116 **sear** (v. i.): dry. 有考证者认为原为 cere up = wear up in cerecloth 涂蜡的裹尸布,即下文的 bonds of death. **embracements**: embraces. **a next**: another wife.

117 **thou**: 旧时第二人称单数代词,此处对指环称呼。

118 **sense**: sensory powers,知觉。

120 **trifles**: love tokens.

121 **still**: always. **win of**: gain from. 言无论身价或赠小礼品,都是 Imogen 方面更高贵。

123 **gods**: 罗马神话中之众神。古不列颠时尚无一神的基督教。

124 **see**: see each other.

125 **Thou**,长辈称晚辈 thou 是正常用法。 **avoid**: leave, begone.

126 **thou**: 此处 Cymbeline 称 Posthumus 为 thou 有轻蔑之意。 **fraught**: burden.

Post. The gods protect you,
And bless the good remainders of the court!
I am gone. [*Exit.*

Imo. There cannot be a pinch in death
More sharp than this is.

Cym. O disloyal thing,
That shouldst repair my youth, thou heap'st
A year's age on me!

Imo. I beseech you, sir,
Harm not yourself with your vexation:
I am senseless of your wrath; a touch more rare
Subdues all pangs, all fears.

Cym. Past grace? obedience?

Imo. Past hope, and in despair; that way, past grace.

Cym. That mightst have had the sole son of my queen!

Imo. O blessed, that I might not! I chose an eagle,
And did avoid a puttock.

Cym. Thou took'st a beggar; wouldst have made my throne
A seat for baseness.

Imo. No; I rather added
A lustre to it.

Cym. O thou vile one!

Imo. Sir,
It is your fault that I have loved Posthumus:
You bred him as my playfellow, and he is
A man worth any woman, overbuys me
Almost the sum he pays.

Cym. What, art thou mad!

Imo. Almost, sir: heaven restore me! Would I were
A neat-herd's daughter, and my Leonatus
Our neighbour-shepherd's son!

Cym. Thou foolish thing!

129 **remainders of**：people remaining at.

130 **pinch**：pain.

132 **repair**：restore. **heap'st**：load. thou 的动词多以-st 或-est 结尾。

135 **am senseless of**：am insensible to，cannot feel. **touch**：sensation，i. e.，sorrow at parting from Posthumus.

136 **grace**：sense of duty.

137 **grace**：blessedness，redemption，这里杂入了一个基督教的神恩的概念。

138 **had**，i. e.，married.

140 **puttock**：鸢，一种低飞的猛禽。

145 **bred him**：brought him up.

146 **overbuys**：pays too much for … by.

148 **heaven restore me**：may heaven cure me (of madness).

149 **neat-herd**：cowherd，牧牛人。

Re-enter Queen.

They were again together: you have done
Not after our command. Away with her,
And pen her up.
Queen. Beseech you Patience. Peace,
Dear lady daughter, peace! Sweet sovereign,
Leave us to ourselves, and make yourself some comfort
Out of your best advice.
Cym. Nay, let her languish
A drop of blood a day; and, being aged,
Die of this folly! [*Exeunt Cymbeline and Lords.*
Queen. Fie! you must give way.

Enter Pisanio.

Here is your servant. How now, sir! What news?
Pis. My lord your son drew on my master.
Queen. Ha!
No harm, I trust, is done?
Pis. There might have been,
But that my master rather play'd than fought,
And had no help of anger: they were parted
By gentlemen at hand.
Queen. I am very glad on 't.
Imo. Your son's my father's friend; he takes his part.
To draw upon an exile! O brave sir!
I would they were in Afric both together;
Myself by with a needle, that I might prick
The goer-back. Why came you from your master?
Pis. On his command: he would not suffer me
To bring him to the haven: left these notes
Of what commands I should be subject to
When 't pleased you to employ me.

152 **after**: according to.

153 **Beseech** 前省略 I. **Peace**: silence.

156 **advice**: deliberate consideration.

156—157 **languish ... day**: 旧时以为人每叹一口气就要失去一滴血。

159 **How now**: what is the matter.

160 **your son**, i. e., Cloten. **drew on**: drew his sword on. **my master**, i. e., Posthumus.

164 **on't**: of it.

165 **his part**: Cymbeline's side.

167 **Afric**: Africa, i. e., some desert spot where no one would stop the combat.

168 **Myself** 前省略 with. **that**: so that.

170 **suffer**: allow.

171 **haven**: harbour.

Queen. This hath been
Your faithful servant: I dare lay mine honour
He will remain so.
Pis. I humbly thank your highness.
Queen. Pray, walk awhile.
Imo. About some half-hour hence,
I pray you, speak with me: you shall at least
Go see my lord aboard: for this time leave me.
[*Exeunt.*

SCENE II

The same. A public place.

Enter Cloten and two Lords.

First Lord. Sir, I would advise you to shift a shirt; the violence of action hath made you reek as a sacrifice; where air comes out, air comes in: there's none abroad so wholesome as that you vent.

Clo. If my shirt were bloody, then to shift it. Have I hurt him?

Sec. Lord. [*Aside*] No, faith; not so much as his patience.

First Lord. Hurt him! his body's a passable carcass, if he be not hurt: it is a thoroughfare for steel, if it be not hurt.

Sec. Lord. [*Aside*] His steel was in debt; it went o' the backside the town.

Clo. The villain would not stand me.

Sec. Lord. [*Aside*] No, but he fled forward still toward your face.

First Lord. Stand you! You have land enough of your own; but he added to your having; gave

174 **lay**：wager.

176 **hence**：from now，later.

178 **this time**：the present.

I. ii.

1 **shift**：change.

2 **reek**：emit vapour，steam.

3 **sacrifice**：祭品。

4 **abroad**：outside（your body）.

6 **to shift it** 前省略 I would be ready.

8 **faith**：in faith，indeed.

10 **passage**：affording free passage.

11 **steel**：sword.

13 **was in debt**：欠了债，为躲债只走背静的小路。

15 **stand**：stand to confront.

16 **still**：always.

you some ground.

Sec. Lord. [*Aside*] As many inches as you have oceans. Puppies!

Clo. I would they had not come between us.

Sec. Lord. [*Aside*] So would I, till you had measured how long a fool you were upon the ground.

Clo. And that she should love this fellow, and refuse me!

Sec. Lord. [*Aside*] If it be a sin to make a true election, she is damned.

First Lord. Sir, as I told you always, her beauty and her brain go not together: she's a good sign, but I have seen small reflection of her wit.

Sec. Lord. [*Aside*] She shines not upon fools, lest the reflection should hurt her.

Clo. Come, I'll to my chamber. Would there had been some hurt done!

Sec. Lord. [*Aside*] I wish not so; unless it had been the fall of an ass, which is no great hurt.

Clo. You'll go with us?

First Lord. I'll attend your lordship.

Clo. Nay, come, let's go together.

Sec. Lord. Well, my lord. [*Exeunt.*

SCENE III

A room in Cymbeline's palace.

Enter Imogen and Pisanio.

Imo. I would thou grew'st unto the shores o' the haven
And question'dst every sail: if he should write
And I not have it, 'twere a paper lost,
As offer'd mercy is. What was the last
That he spake to thee?

21 **As** 前省略 he gave (yielded). **as you have oceans**：as none.

24—25 **measured ... were**：fell flat.

28 **true**：right，correct. **election**：choice.

30 **go not together**：do not match. **'s**：has. **sign**：outward appearance.

31 **small reflection**：little shining. **wit**：intelligence.

33 **reflection**：反射。

34 **to**：go to.

39 **attend**：wait on，accompany.

I. iii.

1 **grew'st unto**：took root on，stayed fixed on.

2 **question'dst**：examined，inquired into. **sail**：ship.

3 **'twere**：it would be. **paper**：document.

4 **As offer'd mercy is**：like an offer of mercy (that is lost).

Pis. It was, his queen, his queen!
Imo. Then waved his handkerchief?
Pis. And kiss'd it, madam.
Imo. Senseless linen! happier therein than I!
And that was all?
Pis. No, madam; for so long
As he could make me with this eye or ear
Distinguish him from others, he did keep
The deck, with glove, or hat, or handkerchief,
Still waving, as the fits and stirs of's mind
Could best express how slow his soul sail'd on,
How swift his ship.
Imo. Thou shouldst have made him
As little as a crow, or less, ere left
To after-eye him.
Pis. Madam, so I did.
Imo. I would have broke mine eye-strings, crack'd them, but
To look upon him, till the diminution
Of space had pointed him sharp as my needle;
Nay, follow'd him, till he had melted from
The smallness of a gnat to air; and then
Have turn'd mine eye, and wept. But, good Pisanio,
When shall we hear from him?
Pis. Be assured, madam,
With his next vantage.
Imo. I did not take my leave of him, but had
Most pretty things to say: ere I could tell him
How I would think on him at certain hours,
Such thoughts and such; or I could make him swear
The shes of Italy should not betray
Mine interest and his honour; or have charged him,
At the sixth hour of morn, at noon, at midnight,
To encounter me with orisons, for then

5 **spake**: spoke.

7 **Senseless**: insensible, unfeeling.

10 **keep**: remain on.

15 **ere left**: before you ceased.

16 **after-eye**: gaze after.

17 **eye-strings**: eye tendons.

17 **but**: only.

19 **Of space**: caused by distance. **pointed ... needle**: made him look as small as a needle point.

21 **air**: unsubstantiality, nothing.

24 **With his next vantage**: at his first opportunity.

29 **shes**: women.

30 **interest**: right, claim.

31 **of morn**: in the morning.

32 **encounter**: meet. **orisons**: prayers.

I am in heaven for him; or ere I could
Give him that parting kiss which I had set
Betwixt two charming words, comes in my father,
And, like the tyrannous breathing of the north,
Shakes all our buds from growing.

Enter a Lady.

Lady. The queen, madam,
Desires your highness' company.
Imo. Those things I bid you do, get them dispatch'd.
I will attend the queen.
Pis. Madam, I shall. [*Exeunt.*

SCENE IV

Rome. Philario's house.

Enter Philario, Iachimo, a Frenchman, a Dutchman, and a Spaniard.

Iach. Believe it, sir, I have seen him in Britain: he was then of a crescent note; expected to prove so worthy as since he hath been allowed the name of: but I could then have looked on him without the help of admiration, though the catalogue of his endowments had been tabled by his side and I to peruse him by items.

Phi. You speak of him when he was less furnished than now he is with that which makes him both without and within.

French. I have seen him in France: we had very many there could behold the sun with as firm eyes as he.

Iach. This matter of marrying his king's daughter, wherein he must be weighed rather by her value

33 **or ere**：before.

35 **comes**：came，用现在时以突出戏剧性。下面 Shakes 同。

36 **breathing**：wind.

I. iv.

1 **him**，i. e.，Posthumus.

2 **crescent note**：growing reputation.

5 **admiration**：wonder and veneration.

6 **tabled**：listed.

7 **by items**：item by item.

9 **makes**：constitutes.

12 **could** 前省略 who. **behold the sun with … firm eyes**：能直视太阳者，指雄鹰，参看 I. i. 139 行，那里 Imogen 把 Posthumus 比作雄鹰。

than his own, words him, I doubt not, a great deal from the matter.

French. And then his banishment.

Iach. Ay, and the approbation of those that weep this lamentable divorce under her colours are wonderfully to extend him; be it but to fortify her judgement, which else an easy battery might lay flat, for taking a beggar without less quality. But how comes it he is to sojourn with you? how creeps acquaintance?

Phi. His father and I were soldiers together; to whom I have been often bound for no less than my life. Here comes the Briton: let him be so entertained amongst you as suits, with gentlemen of your knowing, to a stranger of his quality.

Enter Posthumus.

I beseech you all, be better known to this gentleman; whom I commend to you as a noble friend of mine: how worthy he is I will leave to appear hereafter, rather than story him in his own hearing.

French. Sir, we have known together in Orleans.

Post. Since when I have been debtor to you for courtesies, which I will be ever to pay and yet pay still.

French. Sir, you o'er-rate my poor kindness: I was glad I did atone my countryman and you; it had been pity you should have been put together with so mortal a purpose as then each bore, upon importance of so slight and trivial a nature.

Post. By your pardon, sir, I was then a young traveller; rather shunned to ge even with what I heard than in my every action to be guided by

16 **words**：describes，represents.

16—17 **a great deal from the matter**：wide of the truth，very different from the truth.

19 **weep**：lament.

20 **divorce**：separation. **colours**：banners. **under her colours**：on Imogen's side. **are**，按现代语法应为 is.

21 **extend him**：magnify him，exaggerate his worth. **but**：only. **fortify**：strengthen.

22 **else**：otherwise. **easy battery**，i. e.，slight assault.

23 **taking**：marrying. **without less quality**：of no rank or merit (a kind of double negative).

24 **how comes it**：how does it come about that.

25 **how creeps acquaintance**：how does acquaintance come to be between you so stealthily and unexpectedly.

30 **knowing**：knowledge. **stranger**：foreigner. **quality**：rank.

34 **story** (v. t.)：tell，relate.

36 **known together**：known each other，been acquainted.

38 **ever to pay**：ever ready to pay.

41 **atone**：reconcile.

42 **put together**：set against each other (in a duel).

43 **mortal**：deadly.

44 **importance**：import，a matter.

46 **shunned**：kept far from，refused. **go even with**：agree with.

others' experiences: but upon my mended judgement—if I offend not to say it is mended—my quarrel was not altogether slight.

French. Faith, yes, to be put to the arbitrement of swords, and by such two that would, by all likelihood, have confounded one the other, or have fallen both.

Iach. Can we with manners ask what was the difference?

French. Safely, I think: 'twas a contention in public, which may without contradiction suffer the report. It was much like an argument that fell out last night, where each of us fell in praise of our country mistresses; this gentleman at that time vouching—and upon warrant of bloody affirmation—his to be more fair, virtuous, wise, chaste, constant-qualified and less attemptable than any the rarest of our ladies in France.

Iach. That lady is not now living, or this gentleman's opinion, by this, worn out.

Post. She holds her virtue still and I my mind.

Iach. You must not so far prefer her 'fore ours of Italy.

Post. Being so far provoked as I was in France, I would abate her nothing, though I profess myself her adorer, not her friend.

Iach. As fair and as good—a kind of hand-in-hand comparison—had been something too faire and too good for any lady in Britany. If she went before others I have seen, as that diamond of yours outlustres many I have beheld, I could not but believe she excelled many: but I have not seen the most precious diamond that is, nor you the lady.

49 **mended**: improved.

51—52 **arbitrement of swords**: settlement by duel.

52 第二个 **by**: in.

53 **confounded**: destroyed.

55 **difference**: quarrel, contention.

56 **Safely**: without danger of offence.

57 **contradiction**: objection. **suffer**: allow.

58—59 **fell out**: came to pass, happened.

59 **fell in**: fell into.

60 **country** (adj.): of one's own country.

61—62 **upon warrant … affirmation**: pledging to back it up with a duel.

63 **constant-qualified**: faithful. **attemptable**: seducible.

65 **That**: such a.

66 **this**: now. **worn out**: (is) effaced from mind, rendered useless.

67 **mind**: opinion.

68 **ours**, i. e., our ladies.

71 **abate her nothing**: subtract nothing from my valuation of her.

72 **friend**: lover. 这里是说 adorer 比 lover 客观一些。

73 **fair**: beautiful.

75 **Britany**: Britain.

75—76 **went before**: surpassed.

77 **outlustres**: outshines.

79 **that is**: there is.

Post. I praised her as I rated her: so do I my stone.

Iach. What do you esteem it at?

Post. More than the world enjoys.

Iach. Either your unparagoned mistress is dead, or she's outprized by a trifle.

Post. You are mistaken: the one may be sold or given, if there were wealth enough for the purchase or merit for the gift: the other is not a thing for sale, and only the gift of the gods.

Iach. Which the gods have given you!

Post. Which, by their graces, I will keep.

Iach. You may wear her in title yours: but, you know, strange fowl light upon neighbouring ponds. Your ring may be stolen too: so your brace of unprizable estimations, the one is but frail and the other casual; a cunning thief, or a that way accomplished courtier, would hazard the winning both of first and last.

Post. Your Italy contains none so accomplished a courtier to convince the honour of my mistress; if, in the holding or loss of that, you term her frail. I do nothing doubt you have store of thieves; notwithstanding, I fear not my ring.

Phi. Let us leave here, gentlemen.

Post. Sir, with all my heart. This worthy signior, I thank him, makes no stranger of me; we are familiar at first.

Iach. With five times so much conversation, I should get ground of your fair mistress, make her go back even to the yielding, had I admittance and opportunity to friend.

Post. No, no.

Iach. I dare thereupon pawn the moiety of my estate

81 **rated**: valued.

83 **enjoys**: possesses.

84 **unparagoned**: unparallelled.

85 **outprized**: overvalued.

86 **the one**, i. e., the ring.

88 **the other**, i. e., the lady, Imogen.

93 **wear**: have. **in title**: nominally.

96 **brace**: couple, two objects. **unprizable**: priceless.

97 **casual**: subject to accident.

98 **that way accomplished**, i. e., skilled in seduction and theft. 此复合短语修饰后置的 courtier.

99 **first and last**, i. e., the lady and the ring.

101 **convince**: overcome, defeat.

102 **holding**: keeping. **that**, i. e., her honour.

103 **nothing** (adv.): not at all. **store**: plenty.

104 **fear**: fear for, am anxious for.

105 **leave**: stop the discussion.

107 **makes no stranger of**: does not treat as a stranger.

108 **at first**: from the first.

110 **get ground of**: get the advantage of.

112 **to friend**: for friend, as a friend.

114 **moiety**: half.

to your ring, which in my opinion o'er-values it something: but I make my wager rather against your confidence than her reputation: and, to bar your offence herein too, I durst attempt it against any lady in the world.

Post. You are a great deal abused in too bold a persuasion, and I doubt not you sustain what you're worthy of by your attempt.

Iach. What's that?

Post. A repulse: though your attempt, as you call it, deserve more; a punishment too.

Phi. Gentlemen, enough of this: it came in too suddenly; let it die as it was born, and, I pray you, be better acquainted.

Iach. Would I had put my estate and my neighbour's on the approbation of what I have spoke!

Post. What lady would you choose to assail?

Iach. Yours; whom in constancy you think stands so safe. I will lay you ten thousand ducats to your ring, that, commend me to the court where your lady is, with no more advantage than the opportunity of a second conference, and I will bring from thence that honour of hers which you imagine so reserved.

Post. I will wage against your gold, gold to it: my ring I hold dear as my finger; 'tis part of it.

Iach. You are a friend, and therein the wiser. If you buy ladies' flesh at a million a dram, you cannot preserve it from tainting: but I see you have some religion in you, that you fear.

Post. This is but a custom in your tongue; you bear a graver purpose, I hope.

Iach. I am the master of my speeches, and would undergo what's spoken, I swear.

116 something: somewhat.

117—118 bar your offence: prevent you from feeling personally affronted.

118 durst: dared, would venture to,假设语气。

120 abused: deceived. **persuasion**: conviction.

121 sustain: will receive, will meet with.

121—122 what you're worthy of: what you deserve.

126 came in: was mentioned.

129 Would: I wish.

130 approbation: proof, attestation. **spoke**: spoken.

133 lay: wager. **ducats**:旧时一些欧洲国家通用的金币。

134 commend me: if you give me a letter of introduction.

138 reserved: safely guarded.

139 wage: bet, wager. **to it**: to match it.

142 dram:微小的重量单位。

144 that: since.

148 undergo: undertake.

Post. Will you? I shall but lend my diamond till your return: let there be covenants drawn between's; my mistress exceeds in goodness the hugeness of your unworthy thinking: I dare you to this match: here's my ring.

Phi. I will have it no lay.

Iach. By the gods, it is one. If I bring you no sufficient testimony that I have enjoyed the dearest bodily part of your mistress, my ten thousand ducats are yours; so is your diamond too: if I come off, and leave her in such honour as you have trust in, she your jewel, this your jewel, and my gold are yours; provided I have your commendation for my more free entertainment.

Post. I embrace these conditions; let us have articles betwixt us. Only, thus far you shall answer: if you make your voyage upon her, and give me directly to understand you have prevailed, I am no further your enemy; she is not worth our debate: if she remain unseduced, you not making it appear otherwise, for your ill opinion and the assault you have made to her chastity, you shall answer me with your sword.

Iach. Your hand; a covenant : we will have these things set down by lawful counsel, and straight away for Britain, lest the bargain should catch cold and starve: I will fetch my gold, and have our two wagers recorded.

Post. Agreed. [*Exeunt Posthumus and Iachimo.*

French. Will this hold, think you?

Phi. Signior Iachimo will not from it. Pray let us follow 'em. [*Exeunt.*

154 I will not allow the wager.

162—163 **free entertainment**：ready reception.

164 **embrace**：accept.

165 **answer**：be responsible.

166 **voyage**，i. e.，attempt.

167 **directly**：plainly.

168 **further**：longer.

171 **to**：on.

174 **straight**（adv.）：at once.

175 **away** 前省略 go，即 depart.

176 **starve**：die.

180 **from** 前省略 depart.

SCENE V

Britain. A room in Cymbeline's palace.

Enter Queen, Ladies, and Cornelius.

Queen. Whiles yet the dew's on ground, gather those flowers;
Make haste: who has the note of them?
First Lady. I, madam.
Queen. Dispatch. [*Exeunt Ladies.*
Now, master doctor, have you brought those drugs?
Cor. Pleaseth your highness, ay: here they are, madam:
[*Presenting a small box.*
But I beseech your grace, without offence,—
My conscience bids me ask—wherefore you have
Commanded of me these most poisonous compounds,
Which are the movers of a languishing death,
But, though slow, deadly.
Queen. I wonder, doctor,
Thou ask'st me such a question. Have I not been
Thy pupil long? Hast thou not learn'd me how
To make perfumes? distil? preserve? yea, so
That our great king himself doth woo me oft
For my confections? Having thus far proceeded,—
Unless thou think'st me devilish—is't not meet
That I did amplify my judgement in
Other conclusions? I will try the forces
Of these thy compounds on such creatures as
We count not worth the hanging, but none human,
To try the vigour of them and apply
Allayments to their act, and by them gather
Their several virtues and effects.
Cor. Your highness

I. v.

2 **note**：list.

3 **Dispatch**：make haste.

5 **Pleaseth**：if it pleases. **ay**：yes.

7 **wherefore**：why.

8 **Commanded**：demanded with authority.

9 **movers**：causers.

12 **learn'd**：taught.

15 **confections**：mixtures，medical compounds.

16 **meet**（adj.）：fitting.

17 **judgement**：knowledge.

18 **conclusion**：experiments. **try**：test.

22 **Allayments**：antidotes. **act**：action，operation. **them**，i. e.，these tests.

23 **Their**，i. e.，of the compounds. **several**：respective，individual. **virtues**：powers.

Shall from this practice but make hard your heart:
Besides, the seeing these effects will be
Both noisome and infectious.

Queen. O, content thee.

Enter Pisanio.

[*Aside*] Here comes a flattering rascal; upon him
Will I first work: he's for his master,
And enemy to my son. How now, Pisanio!
Doctor, your service for this time is ended;
Take your own way.

Cor. [*Aside*] I do suspect you, madam;
But you shall do no harm.

Queen. [*To Pisanio*] Hark thee, a word.

Cor. [*Aside*] I do not like her. She doth think she has
Strange lingering poisons: I do know her spirit,
And will not trust one of her malice with
A drug of such damn'd nature. Those she has
Will stupefy and dull the sense awhile;
Which first, perchance, she'll prove on cats and dogs,
Then afterward up higher: but there is
No danger in what show of death it makes,
More than the locking up the spirits a time,
To be more fresh, reviving. She is fool'd
With a most false effect; and I the truer,
So to be false with her.

Queen. No further service, doctor,
Until I send for thee.

Cor. I humbly take my leave. [*Exit.*

Queen. Weeps she still, say'st thou? Dost thou think in time
She will not quench and let instructions enter
Where folly now possesses? Do thou work:
When thou shalt bring me word she loves my son,

25 **the seeing**,处在 seeing 和 the seeing of 的过渡性动名词用法。

26 **noisome**：offensive. **content thee**：set your mind at rest.

32 **Hark thee**：listen. thou 变 thee,在现代英语中最终消失。

33 **doth**：does. th 为英格兰南部方言读音和拼法。

34 **lingering**：killing slowly.

35 **one of her malice**：a person with her malice.

36 **damn'd**：damnable. **Those**，i. e.，the drugs.

38 **prove**：test.

40 **show**：appearance.

41 **locking up the spirits**：suspension of the vital functions. 参见上25 行注。**a time**：for a time.

43 **false**：deceiving. **truer**：more honest.

44 **to be**：for being.

46 **Weeps she**：she weeps. **say'st thou**：do you say.

47 **quench**：become cool. **instructions**：good advice.

I'll tell thee on the instant thou art then
As great as is thy master; greater, for
His fortunes all lie speechless, and his name
Is at last gasp: return he cannot, nor
Continue where he is: to shift his being
Is to exchange one misery with another,
And every day that comes comes to decay
A day's work in him. What shalt thou expect,
To be depender on a thing that leans,
Who cannot be new built, nor has no friends,
So much as but to prop him! [*The Queen drops the box: Pisanio takes it up.*] Thou takest up
Thou know'st not what; but take it for thy labour:
It is a thing I made, which hath the king
Five times redeem'd from death: I do not know
What is more cordial: nay, I prithee, take it;
It is an earnest of a further good
That I mean to thee. Tell thy mistress how
The case stands with her; do't as from thyself.
Think what a chance thou changest on; but think
Thou hast thy mistress still, to boot, my son,
Who shall take notice of thee: I'll move the king
To any shape of thy preferment, such
As thou'lt desire; and then myself, I chiefly,
That set thee on to this desert, am bound
To load thy merit richly. Call my women:
Think on my words. [*Exit Pisanio.*
A sly and constant knave;
Not to be shaked: the agent for his master;
And the remembrancer of her to hold
The hand-fast to her lord. I have given him that
Which, if he take, shall quite unpeople her
Of liegers for her sweet; and which she after,
Except she bend her humour, shall be assured

51 **As great as**: of the same high rank as.

52 **name**: reputation.

54 **shift his being**: change his abode.

56 **decay** (v. t.): destroy.

58 **leans**: inclines towards its fall.

61 **for**: as reward for.

64 **cordial**: restorative.

65 **earnest**: initial payment. **good** (n.): benefit.

66 **mean**: intend to give.

68 **chance**: opportunity. **thou changest on**: on which you can change your service (or fortune).

69 **to boot**: in addition.

70 **move**: incite.

71 **shape**: kind. **preferment**: advancement.

73 **desert** n. [di'zəːt]: action deserving reward.

74 **load**: reward.

75 **sly**: artful. **constant**: faithful. **knave**: servant.

77 **remembrancer**: reminder.

78 **hand-fast**: marriage contract. **that**, i. e., the box of drugs.

79 **unpeople**: deprive.

80 **liegers**: ambassadors. **sweet**: sweetheart, lover. **after** (adv.): at a later time.

81 **Except**: unless. **bend**: alters. **humour**: disposition.

To taste of too.

Re-enter Pisanio with Ladies.

So, so; well done, well done:
The violets, cowslips, and the primroses,
Bear to my closet. Fare thee well, Pisanio;
Think on my words. [*Exeunt Queen and Ladies.*

Pis. And shall do:
But when to my good lord I prove untrue,
I'll choke myself: there's all I'll do for you. [*Exit.*

SCENE VI

The same. Another room in the palace.

Enter Imogen alone.

Imo. A father cruel, and a step-dame false;
A foolish suitor to a wedded lady,
That hath her husband banish'd;—O, that husband!
My supreme crown of grief! and those repeated
Vexations of it! Had I been thief-stol'n,
As my two brothers, happy! but most miserable
Is the desire that's glorious: blest be those,
How mean soe'er, that hath their honest wills,
Which seasons comfort. Who may this be? Fie!

Enter Pisanio and Iachimo.

Pis. Madam, a noble gentleman of Rome,
Comes from my lord with letters.

Iach. Change you, madam?
The worthy Leonatus is in safety,
And greets your highness dearly. [*Presents a letter.*

Imo. Thanks, good sir:
You're kindly welcome.

83 **cowslips**：黄花九轮草。 **primroses**：报春花。

84 **closet**：private chamber.

85 **shall** 前面省略 I.

87 **choke**：kill. **there**：that.

I. vi.

1 **step-dame**：step-mother.

3 **hath**：has had.

4 **crown**，i. e.，height. **repeated**：already enumerated.

6 **happy** 前省略 I would have been.

7 **desire that's glorious**：yearning for excellence and renown.

8 **mean**：low in status. **wills**：desires.

9 **Which**，i. e.，having their honest wills. **seasons**：gives relish to. **Fie**，exclamation of contempt or dislike.

11 Comes 前省略 who. **Change you**：do you change your expression (turn pale).

Iach. [*Aside*] All of her that is out of door most rich!
If she be furnish'd with a mind so rare,
She is alone the Arabian bird, and I
Have lost the wager. Boldness be my friend!
Arm me, audacity, from head to foot!
Or, like the Parthian, I shall flying fight;
Rather, directly fly.

Imo. [*Reads*] 'He is one of the noblest note, to whose kindnesses I am most infinitely tied. Reflect upon him accordingly, as you value your trust—
'LEONATUS.'
So far I read aloud:
But even the very middle of my heart
Is warm'd by the rest, and takes it thankfully.
You are as welcome, worthy sir, as I
Have words to bid you, and shall find it so
In all that I can do.

Iach. Thanks, fairest lady
What, are men mad? Hath nature given them eyes
To see this vaulted arch and the rich crop
Of sea and land, which can distinguish 'twixt
The fiery orbs above and the twinn'd stones
Upon the number'd beach, and can we not
Partition make with spectacles so precious
'Twixt fair and foul?

Imo. What makes your admiration?

Iach. It cannot be i' the eye; for apes and monkeys,
'Twixt two such shes, would chatter this way and
Contemn with mows the other: nor i' the judgement;
For idiots, in this case of favour, would
Be wisely definite: nor i' the appetite;
Sluttery, to such neat excellence opposed,
Should make desire vomit emptiness,

15 **out of door**：external.

16 **so**：as.

17 **Arabian bird**：phoenix，传说中古埃及的凤凰神鸟。

20 **Parthian**：古 Parthian（今伊朗西北部）骑手，以边逃边射箭的战术闻名，类我国旧时的回马枪。

21 **directly**：immediately.

22 **note**：reputation.

23 **tied**：bound，obliged. **Reflect upon**：look on，regard.

27 **middle**：core.

33 **vaulted arch**：sky. **crop**：harvest.

35 **twinn'd**：identical.

36 **number'd**：covered with innumerable pebbles. 此字或为 unnumber'd 之误。

37 **Partition**：discrimination. **spectacles**：organs of sight. **precious**：keen，sensitive.

38 **makes**：causes. **admiration**：wonder.

40 **shes**：women. **this way**：in this way，i. e.，in preference for Imogen.

41 **Contemn**：despise. **mows**：grimaces.

42 **case**：question. **favour**：relative beauty，preference.

44 **neat**：elegant.

45 **emptiness**，i. e.，until it is empty.

Not so allured to feed.
Imo. What is the matter, trow?
Iach. The cloyed will,
That satiate yet unsatisfied desire, that tub
Both fill'd and running, ravening first the lamb,
Longs after for the garbage.
Imo. What, dear sir,
Thus raps you? Are you well?
Iach. Thanks, madam; well.
[*To Pisanio*] Beseech you, sir,
Desire my man's abode where I did leave him:
He's strange and peevish.
Pis. I was going, sir,
To give him welcome. [*Exit.*
Imo. Continues well my lord? His health, beseech you?
Iach. Well, madam.
Imo. Is he disposed to mirth? I hope he is.
Iach. Exceeding pleasant; none a stranger there
So merry and so gamesome: he is call'd
The Briton reveller.
Imo. When he was here
He did incline to sadness, and oft-times
Not knowing why.
Iach. I never saw him sad,
There is a Frenchman his companion, one
An eminent monsieur, that, it seems, much loves
A Gallian girl at home: he furnaces
The thick sighs from him; whiles the jolly Briton,
Your lord, I mean, laughs from's free lungs, cries 'O,
Can my sides hold, to think that man, who knows
By history, report, or his own proof,
What woman is, yea, what she cannot choose
But must be, will his free hours languish for

46 **allured to feed**：tempted to eat.

47 **trow**：trust；do you believe. **cloyed will**：glutted lust.

49 **running**：emptying itself. **ravening**：(like a wolf) devouring.

50 **after for**：after，for.

51 **raps**：transports.

52 **Beseech** 前省略 I.

53 **Desire my man's abode**：ask my servant to stay.

54 **strange**：unfamiliar with the place. **peevish**：irritable.

59 **none a stranger**：none of the foreigners. none 为 not 的强调形式。

60 **gamesome**：sexually playful.

62 **sadness**：seriousness.

65 **monsieur** [法，mə'sjəː]：先生。

66 **Gallian**：法国古称 Gaul(高卢)，Gallian 即 French. **furnaces**：exhales like a furnace.

67 **thick**：frequent.

68 **'s**：his. **free**：unconstrained.

69 **sides**：肚皮。 **Can my sides hold**：我的肚皮能不破吗？意谓我能不笑死吗？

70 **proof**：experience.

72 **will**，主语 man，下接 languish. **languish**：pine away，补语 his free hours. **for**：for the sake of.

Assured bondage?'

Imo. Will my lord say so?

Iach. Ay, madam; with his eyes in flood with laughter
It is a recreation to be by
And hear him mock the Frenchman. But, heavens know,
Some men are much to blame.

Imo. Not he, I hope.

Iach. Not he: but yet heaven's bounty towards him might
Be used more thankfully. In himself 'tis much;
In you, which I account his, beyond all talents,
Whilst I am bound to wonder, I am bound
To pity too.

Imo. What do you pity, sir?

Iach. Two creatures heartily.

Imo. Am I one, sir?
You look on me: what wreck discern you in me
Deserves your pity?

Iach. Lamentable! What,
To hide me from the radiant sun, and solace
I' the dungeon by a snuff?

Imo. I pray you, sir,
Deliver with more openness your answers
To my demands. Why do you pity me?

Iach. That others do,
I was about to say, enjoy your—But
It is an office of the gods to venge it,
Not mine to speak on 't.

Imo. You do seem to know
Something of me, or what concerns me: pray you,—
Since doubting things go ill often hurts more
Than to be sure they do; for certainties
Either are past remedies, or, timely knowing,
The remedy then born,—discover to me

73 Assured: certain. **bondage**,指婚姻约束。

79 himself: his personal endowments. **'tis**, i. e., heaven's bounty is.

80 all talents: all price. talent 是旧时欧洲和中东称金银的重量单位。

84 wreck: loss, ruin.

85 Deserves 前省略 that.

86 solace (v. i.): take comfort.

87 snuff: burning wick of a candle.

89 demands: questions.

92 office: duty, function. **venge**: avenge.

93 on 't: of it.

95 doubting: suspecting.

97 past: beyond. **timely knowing**: knowing the certainties in time.

98 born: thought of. **discover**: reveal.

What both you spur and stop.

Iach. Had I this cheek
To bathe my lips upon; this hand, whose touch,
Whose every touch, would force the feeler's soul
To the oath of loyalty; this object, which
Takes prisoner the wild motion of mine eye,
Fixing it only here; should I, damn'd then,
Slaver with lips as common as the stairs
That mount the Capitol; join gripes with hands
Made hard with hourly falsehood—falsehood, as
With labour; then by-peeping in an eye
Base and unlustrous as the smoky light
That's fed with stinking tallow; it were fit
That all the plagues of hell should at one time
Encounter such revolt.

Imo. My lord, I fear,
Has forgot Britain.

Iach. And himself. Not I
Inclined to this intelligence pronounce
The beggary of his change, but 'tis your graces
That from my mutest conscience to my tongue
Charms this report out.

Imo. Let me hear no more.

Iach. O dearest soul, your cause doth strike my heart
With pity, that doth make me sick! A lady
So fair, and fasten'd to an empery,
Would make the great'st king double, to be partner'd
With tomboys hired with that self exhibition
Which your own coffers yield! with diseased ventures
That play with all infirmities for gold
Which rottenness can lend nature! such boil'd stuff
As well might poison poison! Be revenged,
Or she that bore you was no queen and you
Recoil from your great stock.

99 spur：urge on. **stop**：restrain (as of a horse).

104 Fixing，在 1623 年第一对开本中作 firing (enflaming).

105 Slaver：smear with saliva. **stairs**：step.

106 Capitol：罗马的首山，在此曾挖出人头，上建 Jupiter 神庙，其石阶是千人踩、万人踏的。 **gripes**：grips，claspings.

108 by-peeping：glancing sideways.

109 unlustrous：lacking lustre，dull.

112 Encounter：fall upon. **revolt**：faithlessness.

113 forgot：forgotten. **Not I**：I am not.

114 to，i. e.，to tell. **pronounce** 前省略 which，或者 and.

115 beggary：contemptible nature.

116 conscience：inner knowledge.

117 Charms，主语为 graces，视作单数。charms this report out from ... to ... .

118 cause：case.

120 fasten'd：links. **empery**：empire.

121 double：twice as great. **partner'd**：made to share your rights.

122 tomboys：strumpets，harlots. **self**：very，same. **exhibition**：pension，allowance.

123 ventures：venturesome creatures.

125 Which，i. e.，infirmities，can bestow rottenness on nature. **boil'd stuff**：prostitutes who have taken the sweating treatment for venereal disease.

128 Recoil：fall off，degenerate.

Imo. Revenged!
How should I be revenged? If this be true,—
As I have such a heart that both mine ears
Must not in haste abuse,—if it be true,
How should I be revenged?
Iach. Should he make me
Live like Diana's priest, betwixt cold sheets,
Whiles he is vaulting variable ramps,
In your despite, upon your purse? Revenge it.
I dedicate myself to your sweet pleasure,
More noble than that runagate to your bed,
And will continue fast to your affection,
Still close as sure.
Imo. What ho, Pisanio!
Iach. Let me my service tender on your lips.
Imo. Away! I do condemn mine ears that have
So long attended thee. If thou wert honourable,
Thou wouldst have told this tale for virtue, not
For such an end thou seek'st, as base as strange.
Thou wrong'st a gentleman who is as far
From thy report as thou from honour, and
Solicit'st here a lady that disdains
Thee and the devil alike. What ho, Pisanio!
The king my father shall be made acquainted
Of thy assault: if he shall think it fit
A saucy stranger in his court to mart
As in a Romish stew, and to expound
His beastly mind to us, he hath a court
He little cares for, and a daughter who
He not respects at all. What ho, Pisanio!
Iach. O happy Leonatus! I may say:
The credit that thy lady hath of thee
Deserves thy trust, and thy most perfect goodness
Her assured credit. Blessèd live you long!

130 **As**, i. e., I say "if," for.

131 **abuse**: deceive (my heart by believing what they hear).

133 **Diana's priest**: 罗马神话中月亮和狩猎女神的女祭司 priestess,须为贞洁的处女。

134 **vaulting**: mounting, copulating with. **variable**: various. **ramps**: whores.

135 **In your despite**: in contempt of you. **upon your purse**: with your money.

137 **runagate**: renegade.

138 **fast to**: firmly attached to.

139 **Still**: always. **close**: secret. **as sure**: as I am true.

142 **attended**: gave attention to.

147 **Solicit'st**: make advances to (a lady) for lewd purpose.

150 **assault**: attempt on the chastity of a woman.

151 **mart**: do business.

152 **Romish stew**: Roman brothel.

155 **not respects**: does not respect.

157 **credit**: good opinion.

159 **Blessèd live you long**: may you live long and happy.

A lady to the worthiest sir that ever
Country call'd his! and you his mistress, only
For the most worthiest fit! Give me your pardon.
I have spoke this to know if your affiance
Were deeply rooted, and shall make your lord
That which he is new o'er: and he is one
The truest manner'd, such a holy witch
That he enchants societies into him;
Half all men's hearts are his.

Imo. You make amends.

Iach. He sits 'mongst men like a descended god:
He hath a kind of honour sets him off,
More than a mortal seeming. Be not angry,
Most mighty princess, that I have adventured
To try your taking of a false report, which hath
Honour'd with confirmation your great judgement
In the election of a sir so rare,
Which you know cannot err. The love I bear him
Made me to fan you thus, but the gods made you,
Unlike all others, chaffless. Pray, your pardon.

Imo. All's well, sir: take my power i' the court for yours.

Iach. My humble thanks. I had almost forgot
To entreat your grace but in a small request,
And yet of moment too, for it concerns
Your lord; myself and other noble friends
Are partners in the business.

Imo. Pray, what is 't?

Iach. Some dozen Romans of us, and your lord—
The best feather of our wing—have mingled sums
To buy a present for the emperor;
Which I, the factor for the rest, have done
In France: 'tis plate of rare device and jewels
Of rich and exquisite form, their values great;
And I am something curious, being strange,

160 **sir**：gentleman.

161 **call'd his**：called its own.

162 按正常字序 fit 在 For 之前。

163 **affiance**：confidence.

165 **That which he is**，i. e.，your husband. **new o'er**：afresh again. **one**：alone.

166 **witch**：person who bewitches，charms.

167 **societies**：crowds of people. **into**：to，toward.

170 **sets** 前省略 which.

172 **adventured**：dared.

173 **try**：test. **taking**：reception. **which**，i. e.，your taking ….

175 **election**：choice. **sir**：husband.

176 **Which**：whom，i. e.，Posthumus.

177 **fan**：winnow.

178 **chaffless**：without chaff，perfect.

179 **power**：influence.

180 **forgot**：forgotten.

181 **grace**：favour.

182 **moment**：importance.

186 **mingled**：pooled.

188 **factor**：agent.

189 **plate**：silver tableware.

191 **something**：somewhat. **curious**：anxious. **being strange**：being a stranger here.

To have them in safe stowage: may it please you
To take them in protection?

Imo. Willingly;
And pawn mine honour for their safety: since
My lord hath interest in them, I will keep them
In my bedchamber.

Iach. They are in a trunk,
Attended by my men: I will make bold
To send them to you, only for this night;
I must aboard to-morrow.

Imo. O, no, no.

Iach. Yes, I beseech; or I shall short my word
By lengthening my return. From Gallia
I cross'd the seas on purpose and on promise
To see your grace.

Imo. I thank you for your pains:
But not away to-morrow!

Iach. O, I must, madam:
Therefore I shall beseech you, if you please
To greet your lord with writing, do 't to-night:
I have outstood my time, which is material
To the tender of our present.

Imo. I will write.
Send your trunk to me; it shall safe be kept
And truly yielded you. You're very welcome.

[*Exeunt.*

195 **interest**：share.

197 **Attended**：Guarded.

199 **aboard** 前省略 go.

200 **beseech** 后省略 you. **short**（v. t. ）：fall short of，break.

201 **Gallia**：France.

204 **away** 前省略 go.

207 **outstood**：outstayed.

208 **tender**：offering，presentation.

209 **safe be kept**：be kept safe.

210 **truly**：faithfully. **yielded**：returned to.

ACT II

SCENE I

Britain. Before Cymbeline's palace.

Enter Cloten and two Lords.

Clo. Was there ever man had such luck! when I kissed the jack, upon an up-cast to be hit away! I had a hundred pound on't: and then a whoreson jackanapes must take me up for swearing; as if I borrowed mine oaths of him, and might not spend them at my pleasure.

First Lord. What got he by that? You have broke his pate with your bowl.

Sec. Lord. [*Aside*] If his wit had been like him that broke it, it would have run all out.

Clo. When a gentleman is disposed to swear, it is not for any standers-by to curtail his oaths, ha?

Sec. Lord. No, my lord; [*Aside*] nor crop the ears of them.

Clo. Whoreson dog! I give him satisfaction? Would he had been one of my rank!

Sec. Lord. [*Aside*] To have smelt like a fool.

Clo. I am not vexed more at any thing in the earth: a pox on't! I had rather not be so noble as I am; they dare not fight with me, because of the queen my mother: every Jack-slave hath his bellyful of fighting, and I must go up and down like a cock that nobody can match.

Sec. Lord. [*Aside*] You are cock and capon too;

II. i.

1 **had** 前省略 who.

2 **kissed the jack**：草地滚球戏 bowls 中，将自己的木球滚碰到 jack=target ball，by kiss. **up-cast**：final cast or throw.

3 **on't**：betted on.

4 **whoreson**：bastard. **jackanapes**：Jack-an-apes，ape. **take me up**：rebuke me.

5 **of**：from.

7 **by**：for. **broke**：broken.

8 **pate**：head.

9 **wit**：intelligence，brains.

10 **run all out**，i. e.，like water.

12 **curtail**：cut the tail of a dog，shorten.

13 **crop**：cut short.

15 **give him satisfaction**：give him satisfying (compensation) of honour by a duel.

16 **rank**：(1) 等级，上等人不和下等人决斗；(2) 臭气；双关。

18 **in**：on.

19 **pox**：梅毒。 **noble**：地位高贵。

21 **Jack-slave**：low-born fellow.

22 **bellyful**：as much as satisfying the appetite.

24 **capon**：(1) castrated cock；(2) foolish fellow；(3) cap on；双关。

and you crow, cock, with your comb on.

Clo. Sayest thou?

Sec. Lord. It is not fit your lordship should undertake every companion that you give offence to.

Clo. No, I know that: but it is fit I should commit offence to my inferiors.

Sec. Lord. Ay, it is fit for your lordship only.

Clo. Why, so I say.

First Lord. Did you hear of a stranger that's come to court to-night?

Clo. A stranger, and I not know on 't!

Sec. Lord. [*Aside*] He's a strange fellow himself, and knows it not.

First Lord. There's an Italian come, and 'tis thought, one of Leonatus' friends.

Clo. Leonatus! a banished rascal; and he's another, whatsoever he be. Who told you of this stranger?

First Lord. One of your lordship's pages.

Clo. Is it fit I went to look upon him? Is there no derogation in't?

Sec. Lord. You cannot derogate, my lord.

Clo. Not easily, I think.

Sec. Lord. [*Aside*] You are a fool granted; therefore your issues, being foolish, do not derogate.

Clo. Come, I'll go see this Italian: what I have lost to-day at bowls I'll win to-night of him. Come, go.

Sec. Lord. I'll attend your lordship.

[*Exeunt Cloten and First Lord.*

That such a crafty devil as is his mother
Should yield the world this ass? a woman that
Bears all down with her brain; and this her son
Cannot take two from twenty, for his heart,

25 **comb**：鸡冠；cock's comb，coxcomb，小丑的鸡冠帽。

26 **Sayest thou**：what do you say?

27 **undertake**：take on，challenge to a duel.

28 **companion**：fellow.

29—30 **commit offence to**：assault.

33 **stranger**：foreigner. **that's come**：who is come，who has come.

35 **on 't**：of it.

36 **strange**：alien，指 Cloten 本不是宫廷中人。

40 **another**，i. e.，another rascal.

45 **derogation**：loss of dignity.

46 **You cannot derogate**：（1）you cannot lose your dignity；（2）you have no dignity to lose；双关。

48 **granted**：acknowledged.

49 **issues**，i. e.，words and deeds.

51 **of**：from.

55 **yield the world**：bring forth to the world.

56 **Bears all down**：carries all before her，overcomes everyone.

57 **for his heart**：for the life of him.

And leave eighteen. Alas, poor princess,
Thou divine Imogen, what thou endurest,
Betwixt a father by thy step-dame govern'd,
A mother hourly coining plots, a wooer
More hateful than the foul expulsion is
Of thy dear husband, than that horrid act
Of the divorce he'ld make! The heavens hold firm
The walls of thy dear honour; keep unshaked
That temple, thy fair mind; that thou mayst stand,
To enjoy thy banish'd lord and this great land!

[*Exit.*

SCENE II

Imogen's bedchamber in Cymbeline's palace: a trunk in one corner of it.

Imogen in bed, reading; a Lady attending.

Imo. Who's there? my woman Helen?
Lady. Please you, madam.
Imo. What hour is it?
Lady. Almost midnight, madam.
Imo. I have read three hours then: mine eyes are weak:
Fold down the leaf where I have left: to bed:
Take not away the taper, leave it burning;
And if thou canst awake by four o' the clock,
I prithee, call me. Sleep hath seized me wholly.

[*Exit Lady.*

To your protection I commend me, gods!
From fairies and the tempters of the night
Guard me, beseech ye!

[*Sleeps. Iachimo comes from the trunk.*

Iach. The crickets sing, and man's o'er-labour'd sense
Repairs itself by rest. Our Tarquin thus

62 hateful: deserving hate, odious. **foul**: wicked.

64 divorce: dissolution of marriage. **he'ld**: he would (like to).

67 enjoy, i. e., 重逢丈夫和继承王位。

II. ii.

1 Please you: if it please you, yes.

7 prithee: pray you.

9 fairies: evil spirits.

10 beseech 前省略 I.

12 Our: Roman. **Tarquin**: 传说中罗马塔昆家族第七代,亦即末代国王的儿子 Tarquinius Sextus,他和 Collatinus 打赌,要试探 Collatinus 之妻 Lucrece 的贞洁和忠诚,并恣意奸污 Lucrece 的故事。见莎士比亚早年长诗 The Rape of Lucrece.

Did softly press the rushes, ere he waken'd
The chastity he wounded. Cytherea,
How bravely thou becomest thy bed! fresh lily!
And whiter than the sheets! That I might touch!
But kiss; one kiss! Rubies unparagon'd,
How dearly they do't! 'Tis her breathing that
Perfumes the chamber thus: the flame o' the taper
Bows toward her, and would under-peep her lids
To see the unclosed lights, now canopied
Under those windows, white and azure, laced
With blue of heaven's own tinct. But my design,
To note the chamber: I will write all down:
Such and such pictures; there the window; such
The adornment of her bed; the arras, figures,
Why, such and such; and the contents o' the story.
Ah, but some natural notes about her body
Above ten thousand meaner moveables
Would testify, to enrich mine inventory.
O sleep, thou ape of death, lie dull upon her!
And be her sense but as a monument,
Thus in a chapel lying! Come off, come off:
[*Taking off her bracelet.*
As slippery as the Gordian knot was hard!
'Tis mine; and this will witness outwardly,
As strongly as the conscience does within,
To the madding of her lord. On her left breast
A mole cinque-spotted, like the crimson drops
I' the bottom of a cowslip: here's a voucher,
Stronger than ever law could make: this secret
Will force him think I have pick'd the lock and ta'en
The treasure of her honour. No more. To what end?
Why should I write this down, that's riveted,
Screw'd to my memory? She hath been reading late
The tale of Tereus; here the leaf's turned down

13 rushes：灯芯草。旧时在地毯尚未出现之前，英国有钱人家用灯芯草铺地，脏了再更换。 **ere**：before.

14 chastity：chaste woman. **Cytherea** [si'θiərə]：希腊海中一岛名。希腊罗马神话中，爱和美的女神 Venus 从海上泡沫中诞生，首先登上此岛，故以岛名代 Venus，这里借指 Imogen.

15 bravely：beautifully. **becomest**：befit，suit.

17 unparagon'd：matchless.

18 dearly：exquisitely. **do't**，i. e.，kiss each other.

20 under-peep：peep under. **lids**：eyelids.

21 canopied：covered.

22 windows，i. e.，eyelids. **laced**：adorned with a texture.

23 tinct：hue.

26 arras：tapestry，formerly made at Arras，France. **figures**：carvings.

28 notes：marks.

29 Above：better than. **moveables**：pieces of furniture.

30 inventory：catalogue，list of things.

31 ape：imitation. **dull**：heavy.

32 be her sense：let her senses be. **monument**：effigy on a tomb. 西方教堂石棺上常有的雕像。

34 Gordian knot：传说中小亚细亚 Phrygia 王 Gordius 打了一个复杂的死结，说谁能打开就能统治亚洲，亚历山大大帝一剑就把它砍断了。 **hard**，i. e.，hard to untie.

35 witness：bear testimony.

36 conscience：consciousness.

37 madding：maddening.

38 cinque-spotted：with five spots.

39 cowslip：黄花九轮草，原意为牛粪花。 **voucher**：proof.

41 pick'd the lock，i. e.，have sex with a woman.

45 Tereus：希腊传说中 Thrace 的国王，他强奸了妻妹 Philomela 并割去她的舌头。她把此事织成图画告诉了姐姐，最后自己化作夜莺。

Where Philomel gave up. I have enough:
To the trunk again, and shut the spring of it.
Swift, swift, you dragons of the night, that dawning
May bare the raven's eye! I lodge in fear;
Though this a heavenly angel, hell is here.

[*Clock strikes.*

One, two, three: time, time!

[*Goes into the trunk. The scene closes.*

SCENE III

An ante-chamber adjoining Imogen's apartments.

Enter Cloten and Lords.

First Lord. Your lordship is the most patient man in loss, the most coldest that ever turned up ace.

Clo. It would make any man cold to lose.

First Lord. But not every man patient after the noble temper of your lordship. You are most hot and furious when you win.

Clo. Winning will put any man into courage. If I could get this foolish Imogen, I should have gold enough. It's almost morning, is't not?

First Lord. Day, my lord.

Clo. I would this music would come: I am advised to give her music o' mornings; they say it will penetrate.

Enter Musicians.

Come on; tune: if you can penetrate her with your fingering, so; we'll try with tongue too: if none will do, let her remain; but I'll never give o'er. First, a very excellent good-conceited thing; after, a wonderful sweet air, with admir-

46 **gave up**：was forced to yield.

47 **To** 前省略 go. **spring**：弹簧锁。

48 **dragons of the night**：西方神话中黑夜守卫的怪兽。 **that**：so that.

49 **raven's eye** 喻太阳。

II. iii.

2 **most coldest**，双重最高级，coolest. **ace**：骰子一点为最低点，犹言输了。读音似 ass，笨驴。

3 **cold**：disappointed.

4 **after**：according to.

12 **o'mornings**：of mornings，every morning.

13 **penetrate**：make a deep impression.

17 **o'er**：over，up. **good-conceited**：elaborate and ingenious.

18 **after**：then. **air**：tune.

able rich words to it: and then let her consider.

SONG.

Hark, hark! the lark at heaven's gate sings,
And Phœbus 'gins arise,
His steeds to water at those springs
On chaliced flowers that lies;
And winking Mary-buds begin
To ope their golden eyes;
With every thing that pretty is,
My lady sweet, arise:
Arise, arise!

Clo. So, get you gone. If this penetrate, I will consider your music the better: if it do not, it is a vice in her ears, which horse-hairs and calves'-guts, nor the voice of unpaved eunuch to boot, can never amend. [*Exeunt Musicians.*

Sec. Lord. Here comes the king.

Clo. I am glad I was up so late; for that's the reason I was up so early: he cannot choose but take this service I have done fatherly.

Enter Cymbeline and Queen.

Good morrow to your majesty and to my gracious mother.

Cym. Attend you here the door of our stern daughter? Will she not forth?

Clo. I have assailed her with music, but she vouchsafes no notice.

Cym. The exile of her minion is too new;
She hath not yet forgot him: some more time
Must wear the print of his remembrance out,
And then she's yours.

Queen. You are most bound to the king,

20 **Hark**：listen.

21 **Phœbus** ['fi:bəs]：希腊神话中的太阳神。 **'gins**：begins to.

22 **water**（v. t.）：supply with water to drink，补语为 his steeds.

23 **chaliced**：cup-shaped. **that lies**，修饰上行 springs，视为单数，on 短语为补语。

24 **winking**：closed. **Mary-buds**：buds of marigold，金盏花。

25 **ope**：open.

26 **With**：together with.

30 **consider**：reward.

31 **vice**：defect. **horse-hairs**：bowstrings.

32 **calves'-guts**：fiddlestrings. **nor**：or，双重否定。 **unpaved**：without pavement，without stones（testicles），castrated.

32—33 **to boot**：into the bargain.

35 **was up so late**：stayed awake so long.

38 **Good morrow**：good morning.

40 **Attend**：do homage at. **stern**：hard-hearted.

41 **forth** 前省略 come.

42 **vouchsafes**：grants.

44 **minion**：darling.

45 **forgot**：forgotten.

46 **print**：imprint.

47 **bound**：obliged.

Who lets go by no vantages that may
Prefer you to his daughter. Frame yourself
To orderly soliciting, and be friended
With aptness of the season; make denials
Increase your services; so seem as if
You were inspired to do those duties which
You tender to her; that you in all obey her,
Save when command to your dismission tends,
And therein you are senseless.

Clo. Senseless! not so.

Enter a Messenger.

Mess. So like you, sir, ambassadors from Rome;
The one is Caius Lucius.

Cym. A worthy fellow,
Albeit he comes on angry purpose now;
But that's no fault of his: we must receive him
According to the honour of his sender;
And towards himself, his goodness forespent on us,
We must extend our notice. Our dear son,
When you have given good morning to your mistress,
Attend the queen and us; we shall have need
To employ you towards this Roman. Come, our queen. [*Exeunt all but Cloten.*

Clo. If she be up, I'll speak with her; if not,
Let her lie still and dream. By your leave, ho! [*Knocks.*
I know her women are about her: what
If I do line one of their hands? 'Tis gold
Which buys admittance; oft it doth; yea, and makes
Diana's rangers false themselves, yield up
Their deer to the stand o' the stealer; and 'tis gold
Which makes the true man kill'd and saves the thief;
Nay, sometime hangs both thief and true man: what

48 **vantages**：opportunities.

49 **Prefer**：recommend. **Frame**：conform，prepare.

50 **soliciting**：solicitations. **friended**：assisted，favoured.

51 **With**：by. **aptness of the season**：appropriate timing. **denials**，i. e.，Imogen's refusals.

55 **Save**：except.

56 **senseless**：insensible，pretending not to understand. **Senseless**：stupid.

57 **So like you**：if it pleases you.

59 **Albeit**：although.

61 **his sender**，i. e.，the Pope.

62 **forespent**：previously bestowed.

63 **notice**：attention.

65 **Attend**：come to wait on.

69 **leave**：permission.

71 **line**：fill with money.

73 **Diana's rangers**：为罗马神话中的狩猎女神看守猎物的仙女，均应为处女。 **false themselves**：turn false.

74 **stand**：(1) standing place；(2) erect penis；双关。

75 **true**：honest.

Can it not do and undo? I will make
One of her women lawyer to me, for
I yet not understand the case myself.
By your leave. [*Knocks.*

Enter a Lady.

Lady. Who's there that knocks?
Clo. A gentleman.
Lady. No more?
Clo. Yes, and a gentlewoman's son.
Lady. That's more
Than some whose tailors are as dear as yours
Can justly boast of. What's your lordship's pleasure?
Clo. Your lady's person: is she ready?
Lady. Ay,
To keep her chamber.
Clo. There is gold for you;
Sell me your good report.
Lady. How! my good name? or to report of you
What I shall think is good? The princess!
[*Exit Lady.*

Enter Imogen.

Clo. Good morrow, fairest: sister, your sweet hand.
Imo. Good morrow, sir. You lay out too much pains
For purchasing but trouble: the thanks I give
Is telling you that I am poor of thanks
And scarce can spare them.
Clo. Still I swear I love you.
Imo. If you but said so, 'twere as deep with me:
If you swear still, your recompense is still
That I regard it not.
Clo. This is no answer.

78 **lawyer to**: advocate for.

79 **yet not**: do not yet. **understand**: know how to manage.

83 **dear**: asking a high price. 裁缝要钱高,指衣服华贵。

85 **ready**: (1) dressed; (2) prepared;双关。

88 **name**: reputation.

90 **your sweet hand** 前省略 may I kiss.

91 **lay out**: expend.

94 **scarce**: scarcely.

95 **deep**: solemn, binding.

96 **still**: continually.

Imo. But that you shall not say I yield being silent,
I would not speak. I pray you, spare me: faith,
I shall unfold equal discourtesy
To your best kindness: one of your great knowing
Should learn, being taught, forbearance.
Clo. To leave you in your madness, 'twere my sin:
I will not.
Imo. Fools are not mad folks.
Clo. Do you call me fool?
Imo. As I am mad I do:
If you'll be patient, I'll no more be mad;
That cures us both. I am much sorry, sir,
You put me to forget a lady's manners
By being so verbal: and learn now for all
That I, which know my heart, do here pronounce,
By the very truth of it, I care not for you,
And am so near the lack of charity—
To accuse myself—I hate you; which I had rather
You felt than make't my boast.
Clo. You sin against
Obedience, which you owe your father. For
The contract you pretend with that base wretch,
One bred of alms and foster'd with cold dishes,
With scraps o' the court, it is no contract, none:
And though it be allow'd in meaner parties—
Yet who than he more mean? —to knit their souls
On whom there is no more dependency
But brats and beggary, in self-figured knot;
Yet you are curb'd from that enlargement by
The consequence o' the crown, and must not soil
The precious note of it with a base slave,
A hilding for a livery, a squire's cloth,
A pantler, not so eminent.
Imo. Profane fellow!

98 **But that**: except that; if not to ensure that.
99 **faith**: in faith, indeed.
100 **unfold equal discourtesy**: display discourtesy equal.
101 **knowing**: knowledge.
102 **forbearance**: desisting.
103 **'twere**: it would be.
108 **much**: very.
109 **put**: make, compel.
110 **verbal**: talkative. **for all**: once for all.
111 **which**: who.
116 **For**: as for.
117 **pretend**: claim. **that base wretch**, 指 Posthumus.
120 **meaner**: of lower rank.
123 **self-figured**: self-contracted. **knot**, i. e., marriage.
124 **curb'd**: restrained. **enlargement**: freedom of action.
125 **o' the crown**, i. e., of your being heir to the crown.
126 **note**: distinction.
127 **hilding**: kept servant. **cloth**: livery,仆役的号衣。
128 **pantler**: pantry servant.

Wert thou the son of Jupiter, and no more
But what thou art besides, thou wert too base
To be his groom: thou wert dignified enough,
Even to the point of envy, if 'twere made
Comparative for your virtues to be styled
The under-hangman of his kingdom, and hated
For being preferr'd so well.

Clo. The south-fog rot him!

Imo. He never can meet more mischance than come
To be but named of thee. His meanest garment,
That ever hath but clipp'd his body, is dearer
In my respect than all the hairs above thee,
Were they all made such men. How now, Pisanio!

Enter Pisanio.

Clo. 'His garment!' Now, the devil—

Imo. To Dorothy my woman hie thee presently,—

Clo. 'His garment!'

Imo. I am sprited with a fool,
Frighted and anger'd worse: go bid my woman
Search for a jewel that too casually
Hath left mine arm: it was thy master's: 'shrew me,
If I would lose it for a revenue
Of any king's in Europe! I do think
I saw't this morning: confident I am
Last night 'twas on mine arm; I kiss'd it:
I hope it be not gone to tell my lord
That I kiss aught but he.

Pis. 'Twill not be lost.

Imo. I hope so: go and search. [*Exit Pisanio.*

Clo. You have abused me:
'His meanest garment!'

Imo. Ay, I said so, sir:
If you will make 't an action, call witness to 't.

129 Jupiter：罗马神话中众神之王。

131 his，i. e.，Posthumus's. **thou wert dignified enough**：you were raised in status sufficiently.

132—133 if 'twere made… your virtues：if，commensurate with your qualities，you were.

134 under-hangman：assistant hangman.

135 preferr'd so well：advanced so high. **south-fog**：南风刮来的雾被认为潮热而带有疫病。

137 named of：mentioned by.

138 clipped：embraced.

139 respect：regard. **above thee**：on your head.

142 presently：immediately.

143 sprited with：haunted by.

146 'shrew me：beshrew me，misfortune take me.

152 aught：anyone. **but**：except.

153 so，现在会说 not.

155 action：lawsuit.

Clo. I will inform your father.
Imo. Your mother too:
She 's my good lady, and will conceive, I hope,
But the worst of me. So, I leave you, sir,
To the worst of discontent. [*Exit.*
Clo. I 'll be revenged:
'His meanest garment!' Well. [*Exit.*

SCENE IV

Rome. Philario's house.

Enter Posthumus and Philario.

Post. Fear it not, sir: I would I were so sure
To win the king as I am bold her honour
Will remain hers.
Phi. What means do you make to him?
Post. Not any; but abide the change of time;
Quake in the present winter's state, and wish
That warmer days would come: in these fear'd hopes,
I barely gratify your love; they failing,
I must die much your debtor.
Phi. Your very goodness and your company
O'erpays all I can do. By this, your king
Hath heard of great Augustus: Caius Lucius
Will do 's commission throughly: and I think
He 'll grant the tribute, send the arrearages,
Or look upon our Romans, whose remembrance
Is yet fresh in their grief.
Post. I do believe,
Statist though I am none, nor like to be,
That this will prove a war; and you shall hear
The legions now in Gallia sooner landed
In our not-fearing Britain than have tidings

157 **conceive**: think. **hope**: expect.

II. iv.

1 **would**: wish.

2 **bold**: confident.

3 **means do you make to him**: steps do you take to win his favour.

6 **fear'd**: mixed with fear.

7 **gratify**: repay.

10 **By this**: by now.

11 **Augustus**: 罗马巨头 Octavianus, 27 B.C. 起成为第一个罗马皇帝,称 Augustus Caesar, A.D. 14 逝世。可见本剧发生的事在 A.D. 5—14 年间。

12 **throughly**: thoroughly.

13 **He**, i.e., Cymbeline. **tribute**: 贡金,贡物。罗马入侵不列颠虽已退兵,却命不列颠进贡。 **arrearages**: arrears, overdue payments of tribute.

14 **Or**: or ere, sooner than. **whose remembrance**: of whom the memory.

15 **their**: the Britons'.

16 **Statist**: statesman. **like**: likely.

18 **legions**: 古罗马军团。

Of any penny tribute paid. Our countrymen
Are men more order'd than when Julius Cæsar
Smiled at their lack of skill, but found their courage
Worthy his frowning at: their discipline,
Now mingled with their courages, will make known
To their approvers they are people such
That mend upon the world.

Enter Iachimo.

Phi. See! Iachimo!
Post. The swiftest harts have posted you by land,
And winds of all the corners kiss'd your sails,
To make your vessel nimble.
Phi. Welcome, sir.
Post. I hope the briefness of your answer made
The speediness of your return.
Iach. Your lady
Is one of the fairest that I have look'd upon.
Post. And therewithal the best, or let her beauty
Look through a casement to allure false hearts,
And be false with them.
Iach. Here are letters for you.
Post. Their tenour good, I trus.
Iach. 'Tis very like.
Phi. Was Caius Lucius in the Britain court
When you were there?
Iach. He was expected then,
But not approach'd.
Post. All is well yet.
Sparkles this stone as it was wont? or is 't not
Too dull for your good wearing?
Iach. If I had lost it,
I should have lost the worth of it in gold.
I'll make a journey twice as far, to enjoy

21 **more order'd**：better disciplined. **Julius Cæsar**：裘力斯·凯撒，罗马大将，率远征军于55—54 B. C. 两次入侵不列颠。

25 **their approvers**：those who put them to the test.

25—26 **people such That**：such people as.

26 **mend upon the world**：improve in the world's estimation.

27 **harts**：stags. **posted**：speedily conveyed.

28 **corners**：quarters.

30 **your answer**：the answer you received. **made**：caused.

33 **therewithal**：at the same time.

34 **casement**：window. 妓女常在窗后诱客。

36 **tenour**：sense，purport. **like**：likely.

39 **not** 前省略 had.

40 **stone**：precious stone，gem.

A second night of such sweet shortness which
Was mine in Britain; for the ring is won.

Post. The stone 's too hard to come by.

Iach. Not a whit,
Your lady being so easy.

Post. Make not, sir,
Your loss your sport: I hope you know that we
Must not continue friends.

Iach. Good sir, we must,
If you keep covenant. Had I not brought
The knowledge of your mistress home, I grant
We were to question farther: but I now
Profess myself the winner of her honour,
Together with your ring, and not the wronger
Of her or you, having proceeded but
By both your wills.

Post. If you can make 't apparent
That you have tasted her in bed, my hand
And ring is yours: if not, the foul opinion
You had of her pure honour gains or loses
Your sword or mine, or masterless leaves both
To who shall find them.

Iach. Sir, my circumstances,
Being so near the truth as I will make them,
Must first induce you to believe: whose strength
I will confirm with oath; which, I doubt not,
You 'll give me leave to spare, when you shall find
You need it not.

Post. Proceed.

Iach. First, her bedchamber,—
Where, I confess, I slept not, but profess
Had that was well worth watching,—it was hang'd
With tapestry of silk and silver; the story
Proud Cleopatra, when she met her Roman,

51 **knowledge**, i. e., carnal knowledge, sexual account.

52 **question**: dispute, i. e., duel.

57—58 **hand and ring**,视为单数。

59—60 **gains or loses … mine**: makes one of us the winner, the other the loser, of his sword in a duel.

60 **both**, i. e., both swords.

61 **circumstances**: detailed evidence.

65 **spare**: omit.

68 **that**: what. **watching**: staying awake for.

70 **Cleopatra**: 埃及女王。 **her Roman**: Antony. 故事见莎士比亚剧 Antony and Cleopatra.

And Cydnus swell'd above the banks, or for
The press of boats or pride: a piece of work
So bravely done, so rich, that it did strive
In workmanship and value; which I wonder'd
Could be so rarely and exactly wrought,
Since the true life on 't was—

Post. This is true;
And this you might have heard of here, by me,
Or by some other.

Iach. More particulars
Must justify my knowledge.

Post. So they must,
Or do your honour injury.

Iach. The chimney
Is south the chamber; and the chimney-piece,
Chaste Dian bathing; never saw I figures
So likely to report themselves: the cutter
Was as another nature, dumb; outwent her,
Motion and breath left out.

Post. This is a thing
Which you might from relation likewise reap,
Being, as it is, much spoke of.

Iach. The roof o' the chamber
With golden cherubins is fretted: her andirons—
I had forgot them—were two winking Cupids
Of silver, each on one foot standing, nicely
Depending on their brands.

Post. This is her honour!
Let it be granted you have seen all this,—and praise
Be given to your remembrance—the description
Of what is in her chamber nothing saves
The wager you have laid.

Iach. Then, if you can,
[*Showing the bracelet.*

71 Cydnus：古 Cilicia 国(今土耳其中南部)首都 Tarsus 城旁一河名，Cleopatra 曾泛舟此河上。事见上述莎剧二幕二场 190 行以下。**or for**：either because of.

72 piece of work，指 tapestry.

73 bravely：splendidly.

79 justify：confirm.

80 chimney：fireplace.

81 south：in the south of. **chimney-piece**：carving above the fireplace.

82 Dian：Diana，罗马神话中的月亮和狩猎女神。

83 So likely to report themselves：so lifelike that they could give an account of themselves. **cutter**：carver.

84 dumb 前省略 though. **outwent her**：surpassed nature.

86 relation：report. **reap**：gather.

87 spoke：spoken.

88 cherubins：cherubs，小天使，形象为长翅的光身小男孩，有时只露头部。 **fretted**：carved. **andirons**：壁炉中用的柴架。

89 forgot：forgotten. **winking**：blind.

90 nicely：ingeniously.

91 Depending：leaning. **brands**：torches.

93 remembrance：power of memory.

94 nothing (adv.)：not at all. **saves**：preserves，rescues.

Be pale: I beg but leave to air this jewel; see!
And now 'tis up again: it must be married
To that your diamond; I 'll keep them.

Post. Jove!
Once more let me behold it: is it that
Which I left with her?

Iach. Sir,—I thank her—that:
She stripp'd it from her arm; I see her yet;
Her pretty action did outsell her gift,
And yet enrich'd it too: she gave it me
And said she prized it once.

Post. May be she pluck'd it off
To send it me.

Iach. She writes so to you, doth she?

Post. O, no, no, no! 'tis true. Here, take this too;
[*Gives the ring.*
It is a basilisk unto mine eye,
Kills me to look on 't. Let there be no honour
Where there is beauty; truth, where semblance; love,
Where there 's another man: the vows of women
Of no more bondage be to where they are made
Than they are to their virtues; which is nothing.
O, above measure false!

Phi. Have patience, sir,
And take your ring again; 'tis not yet won:
It may be probable she lost it, or
Who knows if one of her women, being corrupted,
Hath stol'n it from her?

Post. Very true;
And so, I hope, he came by 't. Back my ring:
Render to me some corporal sign about her
More evident than this; for this was stol'n.

Iach. By Jupiter, I had it from her arm.

Post. Hark you, he swears; by Jupiter he swears.

96 **pale**：unmoved，not turning red. **leave**：permission. **air**：show.

97 **up**：put away.

98 **Jove**：Jupiter 的别名，罗马神话中的众神之王。

102 **outsell**：exceed in value.

107 **basilisk**：神话中的蛇妖，其目光可以杀人。

108 **no**，此否定词管 honour，truth，love 三名词。

109 **semblance**：mere appearance of truth.

110 **the vows** 前省略 let.

111 **be** 的逻辑主语位置在此行 Of 之前。 **where**：those to whom.

113 **above measure**：immensely.

118 **Back** 前省略 give.

120 **evident**：conclusive.

'Tis true:—nay, keep the ring—'tis true: I am sure
She would not lose it: her attendants are
All sworn and honourable:—they induced to steal it?
and by a stranger! —No, he hath enjoy'd her:
The cognizance of her incontinency
Is this: she hath bought the name of whore thus dearly,
There, take thy hire; and all the fiends of hell
Divide themselves between you!

Phi. Sir, be patient:
This is not strong enough to be believed
Of one persuaded well of—

Post. Never talk on 't;
She hath been colted by him.

Iach. If you seek
For further satisfying, under her breast—
Worthy the pressing—lies a mole, right proud
Of that most delicate lodging: by my life,
I kiss'd it, and it gave me present hunger
To feed again, though full. You do remember
This stain upon her?

Post. Ay, and it doth confirm
Another stain, as big as hell can hold,
Were there no more but it.

Iach. Will you hear more?

Post. Spare your arithmetic; never count the turns;
Once, and a million!

Iach. I 'll be sworn—

Post. No swearing.
If you will swear you have not done 't you lie,
And I will kill thee if thou dost deny
Thou 'st made me cuckold.

Iach. I 'll deny nothing.

Post. O, that I had her here, to tear her limb-meal!
I will go there and do 't; i' the court; before

127 **cognizance**：token，badge.

129 **hire**：fee，i. e.，the ring.

132 **persuaded**：thought. **on't**：of it.

133 **colted**：mounted，sexually enjoyed.

139 **stain**：spot.

142 **turns**：bouts of love-making.

146 **cuckold**：乌龟，奸妇的丈夫。

147 **limb-meal**：limb by limb.

Her father. I 'll do something— [*Exit.*

Phi. Quite besides
The government of patience! You have won:
Let 's follow him and pervert the present wrath
He hath against himself.

Iach. With all my heart. [*Exeunt.*

SCENE V

Another room in Philario's house.

Enter Posthumus.

Post. Is there no way for men to be, but women
Must be half-workers? We are all bastards;
And that most venerable man which I
Did call my father, was I know not where
When I was stamp'd; some coiner with his tools
Made me a counterfeit: yet my mother seem'd
The Dian of that time: so doth my wife
The nonpareil of this. O, vengeance, vengeance!
Me of my lawful pleasure she restrain'd,
And pray'd me oft forbearance; did it with
A pudency so rosy, the sweet view on 't
Might well have warm'd old Saturn; that I thought her
As chaste as unsunn'd snow. O, all the devils!
This yellow Iachimo, in an hour,—was 't not?—
Or less,—at first?—perchance he spoke not, but
Like a full-acorn'd boar, a German one,
Cried 'O!' and mounted; found no opposition
But what he look'd for should oppose and she
Should from encounter guard. Could I find out
The woman's part in me! For there 's no motion
That tends to vice in man but I affirm
It is the woman's part: be it lying, note it,

149 besides: beyond.

150 government: control.

151 pervert: divert.

II. v.

1 be: exist.

2 half-workers: collaborators (in procreation).

3 which: whom.

5 stamp'd: conceived, as coins are stamped.

8 nonpareil: paragon, one who has no equal. **of**: in.

11 pudency: modesty. **on 't**: of it.

12 Saturn: 希腊神话中众神之父 Zeus 之父，后被 Zeus 取而代之。Saturn 是象征"时间"的老翁。

14 yellow: sallow.

15 at first: right away.

16 full-acorn'd: fed full of acorns. **boar**: (1) 公猪；(2) 日耳曼农民。

20 motion: impulse.

The woman's; flattering, hers; deceiving, hers;
Lust and rank thoughts, hers, hers; revenges, hers;
Ambitions, covetings, change of prides, disdain,
Nice longing, slanders, mutability,
All faults that may be named, nay, that hell knows,
Why, hers, in part or all, but rather all;
For even to vice
They are not constant, but are changing still
One vice, but of a minute old, for one
Not half so old as that. I 'll write against them,
Detest them, curse them: yet 'tis greater skill
In a true hate, to pray they have their will:
The very devils cannot plague them better. [*Exit.*

24 **rank**: lascivious.

25 **change of prides**: one extravagance after another.

26 **Nice longing**: wanton appetite.

27 **nay**: indeed.

30 **still**: always.

31 **but of**: only.

33 **skill**: cleverness, sagacity.

34 **hate**: hatred. **will**: desire.

ACT III

SCENE I

Britain. A hall in Cymbeline's palace.

Enter in state, Cymbeline, Queen, Cloten, and Lords at one door, and at another, Caius Lucius, and Attendants.

Cym. Now say, what would Augustus Cæsar with us?
Luc. When Julius Cæsar, whose remembrance yet
Lives in men's eyes and will to ears and tongues
Be theme and hearing ever, was in this Britain
And conquer'd it, Cassibelan, thine uncle,—
Famous in Cæsar's praises, no whit less
Than in his feats deserving it—for him
And his succession granted Rome a tribute,
Yearly three thousand pounds; which by thee lately
Is left untender'd.
Queen. And, to kill the marvel,
Shall be so ever.
Clo. There be many Cæsars
Ere such another Julius. Britain is
A world by itself, and we will nothing pay
For wearing our own noses.
Queen. That opportunity,
Which then they had to take from 's, to resume
We have again. Remember, sir, my liege,
The kings your ancestors, together with
The natural bravery of your isle, which stands
As Neptune's park, ribbed and paled in
With rocks unscaleable and roaring waters,

III. i.

8 **succession**：successors.

10 **kill the marvel**：put an end to the surprise (by making non-payment the rule).

11 **be**：will be.

15 **from 's**：from us. **resume**：take back.

16 **liege**：sovereign.

18 **bravery**：defiance. **isle**：island，i. e. Britain.

19 **Neptune**：罗马神话中的海神。 **ribbed**：enclosed (with ribs).

With sands that will not bear your enemies' boats,
But suck them up to the topmost. A kind of conquest
Cæsar made here; but made not here his brag
Of 'Came, and saw, and overcame': with shame—
The first that ever touch'd him—he was carried
From off our coast, twice beaten; and his shipping—
Poor ignorant baubles! —on our terrible seas,
Like egg-shells moved upon their surges, crack'd
As easily 'gainst our rocks: for joy whereof
The famed Cassibelan, who was once at point—
O giglot fortune! —to master Cæsar's sword,
Made Lud's town with rejoicing fires bright
And Britons strut with courage.

Clo. Come, there 's no more tribute to be paid: out kingdom is stronger than it was at that time: and, as I said, there is no moe such Cæsars: other of them may have crooked noses, but to owe such straight arms, none.

Cym. Son, let your mother end.

Clo. We have yet many among us can gripe as hard as Cassibelan: I do not say I am one; but I have a hand. Why tribute? why should we pay tribute? If Cæsar can hide the sun from us with a blanket, or put the moon in his pocket, we will pay him tribute for light; else, sir, no more tribute, pray you now.

Cym. You must know,
Till the injurious Romans did extort
This tribute from us, we were free: Cæsar's ambition,
Which swell'd so much that it did almost stretch
The sides o' the world, against all colour here
Did put the yoke upon 's; which to shake off
Becomes a warlike people, whom we reckon
Ourselves to be.

23 **brag**: boast.

24 **Came, and saw, and overcame**,主语 I 省略,拉丁文为 veni, vidi, vici.

25 **touch'd**: hurt, struck.

26 **shipping**: ships.

27 **ignorant**: silly. **baubles**: toys, trifles.

30 **at point**: ready, on the point of.

31 **giglot**: giddy, fickle.

32 **Lud's town**: London, Lud 是 Cymbeline 的祖父。旧史误认为伦敦是 Lud 始建的。

36 **moe**: more.

37 **other**: others.

37—38 **to owe**: as regards owning.

38 **straight**: strong.

39 **end**: finish.

40 **can** 前面省略 who. **gripe**: grip.

48 **injurious**: insulting.

51 **sides**: 肚皮。 **against all colour**: without any pretense of right.

53 **Becomes**: befits.

Clo. and Lords. We do.

Cym. Say then to Cæsar,
Our ancestor was that Mulmutius which
Ordain'd our laws, whose use the sword of Cæsar
Hath too much mangled; whose repair and franchise
Shall, by the power we hold, be our good deed,
Though Rome be therefore angry. Mulmutius made our laws,
Who was the first of Britain which did put
His brows within a golden crown, and call'd
Himself a king.

Luc. I am sorry, Cymbeline,
That I am to pronounce Augustus Cæsar—
Cæsar, that hath moe kings his servants than
Thyself domestic officers—thine enemy;
Receive it from me, then: war and confusion
In Cæsar's name pronounce I 'gainst thee: look
For fury not to be resisted. Thus defied,
I thank thee for myself.

Cym. Thou art welcome, Caius.
Thy Cæsar knighted me; my youth I spent
Much under him; of him I gather'd honour;
Which he to seek of me again perforce,
Behoves me keep at utterance. I am perfect
That the Pannonians and Dalmatians for
Their liberties are now in arms; a precedent
Which not to read would show the Britons cold:
So Cæsar shall not find them.

Luc. Let proof speak.

Clo. His majesty bids you welcome. Make pastime with us a day or two, or longer: if you seek us afterwards in other terms, you shall find us in our salt-water girdle: if you beat us out of it, it is yours; if you fall in the adventure, our

55 Mulmutius，据英国古代史家 Holinshed 说，是不列颠第一个国王。

56 whose use：the practice of which.

57 repair：restoration. **franchise**：free exercise.

66 confusion：destruction.

68 defied：challenged；having issued the challenge.

71 of：from. 下行同。

72 to seek of me again：seeking to take back from me. **perforce**：by force.

73 Behoves me keep：it is fit or necessary for me to defend. **at utterance**：to the utmost，to the death. **perfect**：fully aware，fully informed.

74 Pannonians：旧时匈牙利西部 Pannonia 人。 **Dalmatians**：旧时克罗地亚称 Dalmatia，该地居民。

76 cold：lacking in spirit.

77 So，位置在本句末。 **proof**：the result.

78 pastime：amusement.

81 our salt-water girdle：the sea that encircles us.

crows shall fare the better for you; and there 's an end.

Luc. So, sir.

Cym. I know your master's pleasure, and he mine:
All the remain is 'Welcome.' [*Exeunt.*

SCENE II

Another room in the palace.

Enter Pisanio, with a letter.

Pis. How! of adultery? Wherefore write you not
What monster 's her accuser? Leonatus!
O master! what a strange infection
Is fall'n into thy ear! What false Italian,
As poisonous-tongued as handed, hath prevail'd
On thy too ready hearing? Disloyal! No:
She 's punish'd for her truth, and undergoes,
More goddess-like than wife-like, such assaults
As would take in some virtue. O my master!
Thy mind to her is now as low as were
Thy fortunes. How! That I should murder her?
Upon the love and truth and vows which I
Have made to thy command? I, her? Her blood?
If it be so to do good service, never
Let me be counted serviceable. How look I,
That I should seem to lack humanity
So much as this fact comes to? [*Reading*] 'Do 't: the letter
That I have sent her, by her own command
Shall give thee opportunity.' O damn'd paper!
Black as the ink that 's on thee! Senseless bauble,
Art thou a feodary for this act, and look'st
So virgin-like without? Lo, here she comes.

87 **All the remain** (n.): all that is left to say.

III. ii.

2 **'s**: is.

4 **Is fall'n**: has fallen.

5 **handed**, i. e., poisonous-handed, having poisonous hands.

7 **truth**: fidelity. **undergoes**: endures, hold out against.

9 **take in**: overcome, conquer.

10 **to her**: compared to hers.

12 **Upon**: in consequence of.

17 **fact**: action.

20 **Senseless bauble**: insentient trifle.

21 **feodary**: accomplice.

I am ignorant in what I am commanded.

Enter Imogen.

Imo. How now, Pisanio!
Pis. Madam, here is a letter from my lord.
Imo. Who? thy lord? that is my lord Leonatus!
O, learn'd indeed were that astronomer
That knew the stars as I his characters;
He 'ld lay the future open. You good gods,
Let what is here contain'd relish of love,
Of my lord's health, of his content, yet not
That we two are asunder; let that grieve him:
Some griefs are medicinable; that is one of them,
For it doth physic love: of his content,
All but in that! Good wax, thy leave. Blest be
You bees that make these locks of counsel! Lovers
And men in dangerous bonds pray not alike:
Though forfeiters you cast in prison, yet
You clasp young Cupid's tables. Good news, gods!
[*Reads*] 'Justice, and your father's wrath, should he take me in his dominion, could not be so cruel to me, as you, O the dearest of creatures, would even renew me with your eyes. Take notice that I am in Cambria, at Milford-Haven: what your own love will out of this advise you, follow. So he wishes you all happiness, that remains loyal to his vow, and your, increasing in love,

'LEONATUS POSTHUMUS.'

O, for a horse with wings! Hear'st thou, Pisanio?
He is at Milford-Haven: read, and tell me
How far 'tis thither. If one of mean affairs
May plod it in a week, why may not I
Glide thither in a day? Then, true Pisanio,—

23 **am ignorant in**: shall pretend ignorance of.

27 **astronomer**: astrologer.

28 **characters**: handwriting.

30 **relish**: taste.

33 **are medicinable**: have medicinal value.

34 **physic** (v. t.): nurture, strengthen.

35 **thy leave**: your permission. 当时的信用蜂蜡封口;开信破蜡,求其允许。玩笑口吻。

36 **of counsel**: for private matters.

37 **in dangerous bonds**: bound by risky contracts (also sealed with wax).

38 **forfeiters**: those who default on contracts.

39 **clasp**: embrace. **tables**: writing tables, letters.

41 **his dominion**: territory under his rule.

42 **as**: but that, as you would not.

43 **renew**: revive. **with your eyes**, i. e., by seeing me.

44 **Cambria**: Wales. **Milford-Haven**: 威尔士西南角海港。

45 **out of this**: from learning this message.

50 **for**, expressing eagerness to come by.

52 **of mean affairs**: with unimportant business.

Who long'st, like me, to see thy lord; who long'st
O, let me bate,—but not like me—yet long'st
But in a fainter kind:—O, not like me;
For mine 's beyond beyond: say, and speak thick,—
Love's counsellor should fill the pores of hearing,
To the smothering of the sense—how far it is
To this same blessed Milford: and by the way
Tell me how Wales was made so happy as
To inherit such a haven: but, first of all,
How we may steal from hence: and for the gap
That we shall make in time, from our hence-going
And our return, to excuse: but first, how get hence.
Why should excuse be born or ere begot!
We 'll talk of that hereafter. Prithee, speak,
How many score of miles may we well ride
'Twixt hour and hour?

Pis. One score 'twixt sun and sun,
Madam, 's enough for you, and too much too.

Imo. Why, one that rode to 's execution, man,
Could never go so slow: I have heard of riding wagers,
Where horses have been nimbler than the sands
That run i' the clock's behalf. But this is foolery:
Go bid my woman feign a sickness, say
She 'll home to her father: and provide me presently
A riding-suit, no costlier than would fit
A franklin's housewife.

Pis. Madam, you 're best consider.

Imo. I see before me, man: nor here, nor here,
Nor what ensues, but have a fog in them,
That I cannot look through. Away, I prithee;
Do as I bid thee: there 's no more to say;
Accessible is none but Milford way. [*Exeunt.*

56 bate：abate，moderate（my speech）.

58 thick（adv.）：quickly.

59 pores of hearing：ears.

60 sense，i. e.，sense of hearing.

61 by：on.

65 hence-going：departure.

66 And，应为 till. **to excuse**，位置应在 64 行 for the gap 之前。此处 Imogen 情急，说话颠三倒四。

67 be born or ere begot：be produced before（the way of escape）is conceived.

70 'Twixt hour and hour：in an hour. **'twixt sun and sun**：between sunrise and sunset.

71 's：it is.

73 riding：racing.

75 i' the clock's behalf：to serve the purpose of a clock，i. e. in an hourglass.

77 home 前省略 go.

78 fit：suit.

79 franklin：freeholder. 英国旧时的自由农。 **you're best**：you had better.

80 before：straight ahead of. **nor here，nor here**：neither（what is）on this side，nor on that.

SCENE III

Wales: a mountainous country with a cave.

Enter Belarius, Guiderius, and Arviragus.

Bel. A goodly day not to keep house with such
Whose roof 's as low as ours! Stoop, boys: this gate
Instructs you how to adore the heavens, and bows you
To a morning's holy office: the gates of monarchs
Are arch'd so high that giants may jet through
And keep their impious turbans on, without
Good morrow to the sun. Hail, thou fair heaven!
We house i' the rock, yet use thee not so hardly
As prouder livers do.

Gui. Hail, heaven!

Arv. Hail, heaven!

Bel. Now for our mountain sport: up to yond hill!
Your legs are young: I 'll tread these flats. Consider,
When you above perceive me like a crow,
That it is place which lessens and sets off:
And you may then revolve what tales I have told you
Of courts, of princes, of the tricks in war:
That service is not service, so being done,
But being so allow'd: to apprehend thus,
Draws us a profit from all things we see;
And often, to our comfort, shall we find
The sharded beetle in a safer hold
Than is the full-wing'd eagle. O, this life
Is nobler than attending for a check,
Richer than doing nothing for a bauble,
Prouder than rustling in unpaid-for silk:
Such gain the cap of him that makes 'em fine,
Yet keeps his book uncross'd: no life to ours.

III. iii.

1 **goodly**：fine. **keep house**：stay indoors.

3 **bows you**：makes you bow down.

4 **holy office**：prayer.

5 **jet**：stalk，strut.

6 **turbans**：Saracens，即阿拉伯伊斯兰教徒的头巾。因基督教视伊斯兰教为异教，故称 impious.

8 **house**（v. i.)：dwell. **use … hardly**：treat badly.

9 **prouder livers**：those who live more grandly.

11 **flats**：low flat ground.

12 **like**：as small as.

13 **place**：position. **sets off**：enhances.

14 **revolve**：turn over in mind.

17 **allow'd**：acknowledged（by superiors). **apprehend**：understand.

20 **sharded**：长鞘翅的。 **hold**：stronghold，refuge.

22 **attending for a check**：waiting on people only to be rebuked.

23 **bauble**：foolish，childish person.

25 **Such gain**：such men win. **cap**：taking off the cap，deference. **him**，i. e.，the tailor.

26 **book**：account book recording debts. **uncross'd**：uncancelled. **to**：compared to.

Gui. Out of your proof you speak: we, poor unfledged,
Have never wing'd from view o' the nest, nor know not
What air 's from home. Haply this life is best
If quiet life be best, sweeter to you
That have a sharper known, well corresponding
With your stiff age: but unto us it is
A cell of ignorance, travelling a-bed,
A prison for a debtor that not dares
To stride a limit.
Arv. What should we speak of
When we are old as you? when we shall hear
The rain and wind beat dark December, how
In this our pinching cave shall we discourse
The freezing hours away? We have seen nothing:
We are beastly; subtle as the fox for prey,
Like warlike as the wolf for what we eat:
Our valour is to chase what flies; our cage
We make a quire, as doth the prison'd bird,
And sing our bondage freely.
Bel. How you speak!
Did you but know the city's usuries,
And felt them knowingly: the art o' the court,
As hard to leave as keep; whose top to climb
Is certain falling, or so slippery that
The fear 's as bad as falling: the toil o' the war,
A pain that only seems to seek out danger
I' the name of fame and honour, which dies i' the search,
And hath as oft a slanderous epitaph
As record of fair act; nay, many times,
Doth ill deserve by doing well; what 's worse,
Must court'sy at the censure:—O boys, this story
The world may read in me: my body 's mark'd
With Roman swords, and my report was once

27 **proof**: experience.

29 **from**: away from. **Haply**: perhaps.

31 **sharper**, i. e., harsher life.

32 **stiff**: rigid (in limbs).

33 **a-bed**: asleep, while dreaming.

35 **stride**: step over. **limit**: boundary, sanctuary,越出则欠债人将被捕。

38 **pinching**: afflicting with cold.

40 **beastly**: like beasts. **subtle**: cunning.

41 **Like**: as.

43 **quire**: choir,教堂内唱诗班坐区。

46 **art**: artifice.

47 **keep**: stay in.

50 **pain**: labour.

54 **ill deserve**: earn ill treatment.

57 **report**: reputation.

First with the best of note: Cymbeline loved me;
And when a soldier was the theme, my name
Was not far off: then was I as a tree
Whose boughs did bend with fruit: but in one night,
A storm, or robbery, call it what you will,
Shook down my mellow hangings, nay, my leaves,
And left me bare to weather.

Gui. Uncertain favour!

Bel. My fault being nothing, as I have told you oft,
But that two villains, whose false oaths prevail'd
Before my perfect honour, swore to Cymbeline
I was confederate with the Romans; so
Follow'd my banishment; and this twenty years
This rock and these demesnes have been my world:
Where I have lived at honest freedom, paid
More pious debts to heaven than in all
The fore-end of my time. But up to the mountains!
This is not hunters' language: he that strikes
The venison first shall be the lord o' the feast;
To him the other two shall minister;
And we will fear no poison, which attends
In place of greater state. I 'll meet you in the valleys.
[*Exeunt Guiderius and Arviragus.*
How hard it is to hide the sparks of nature!
These boys know little they are sons to the kings;
Nor Cymbeline dreams that they are alive.
They think they are mine: and though train'd up thus meanly
I' the cave wherein they bow, their thoughts do hit
The roofs of palaces, and nature prompts them
In simple and low things to prince it much
Beyond the trick of others. This Polydore,
The heir of Cymbeline and Britain, who
The king his father call'd Guiderius,—Jove!

58 **best of note**: most renowned.

63 **hangings**, i. e., fruit.

67 **Before**: over.

70 **demesnes** [di'meinz]: regions.

71 **at**: in.

73 **fore-end**: early part.

76 **minister**: serve.

77 **attends**: is always present.

82 **meanly**: in a humble style.

85 **prince it**: act like princes.

86 **trick**: manner, habit.

88 **Jove**: by Jove, a mild oath.

When on my three-foot stool I sit and tell
The warlike feats I have done, his spirits fly out
Into my story: say 'Thus mine enemy fell,
And thus I set my foot on 's neck,' even then
The princely blood flows in his cheek, he sweats,
Strains his young nerves, and puts himself in posture
That acts my words. The younger brother, Cadwal,
Once Arviragus, in as like a figure
Strikes life into my speech and shows much more
His own conceiving. Hark, the game is roused!
O Cymbeline! Heaven and my conscience knows
Thou didst unjustly banish me: whereon,
At three and two years old, I stole these babes,
Thinking to bar thee of succession as
Thou reft'st me of my lands. Euriphile,
Thou wast their nurse; they took thee for their mother,
And every day do honour to her grave:
Myself, Belarius, that am Morgan call'd
They take for natural father. The game is up. [*Exit.*

SCENE IV

Country near Milford-Haven.

Enter Pisanio and Imogen.

Imo. Thou told'st me, when we came from horse, the place
Was near at hand: ne'er long'd my mother so
To see me first, as I have now. Pisanio! man!
Where is Posthumus? What is in thy mind,
That makes thee stare thus? Wherefore breaks that sigh
From the inward of thee? One but painted thus
Would be interpreted a thing perplex'd
Beyond self-explication: put thyself

94 nerves：sinews.

96 in as like a figure：in a similar manner.

98 conceiving：imagination. **game**：猎物。此时间打猎的号角声。

103 reft'st：deprived.

107 up：on foot，in motion.

III. iv.

1 came from horse：dismounted.

3 first：初生。 **have**：do.

7 perplex'd：distressed.

Into a haviour of less fear, ere wildness
Vanquish my staider senses. What 's the matter?
Why tender'st thou that paper to me, with
A look untender? If 't be summer news,
Smile to 't before; if wintry, thou need'st
But keep that countenance still. My husband's hand!
That drug-damn'd Italy hath out-craftied him,
And he 's at some hard point. Speak, man: thy tongue
May take of some extremity, which to read
Would be even mortal to me.

Pis. Please you, read;
And you shall find me, wretched man, a thing
The most disdain'd of fortune.

Imo. [*Reads*] 'Thy mistress, Pisanio, hath played the strumpet in my bed; the testimonies whereof lie bleeding in me. I speak not out of weak surmises; but from proof as strong as my grief, and as certain as I expect my revenge. That part thou, Pisanio, must act for me, if thy faith be not tainted with the breach of hers. Let thine own hands take away her life: I shall give thee opportunity at Milford-Haven: she hath my letter for the purpose: where, if thou fear to strike, and to make me certain it is done, thou art the pandar to her dishonour, and equally to me disloyal.'

Pis. What shall I need to draw my sword? the paper
Hath cut her throat already. No, 'tis slander;
Whose edge is sharper than the sword; whose tongue
Outvenoms all the worms of Nile; whose breath
Rides on the posting winds, and doth belie
All corners of the world: kings, queens, and states,
Maids, matrons, nay, the secrets of the grave
This viperous slander enters. What cheer, madam?

9 **haviour**: behaviour. **of less fear**: less fearsome. **ere**: before. **wildness**: madness.

12 **untender**: unkind.

13 **before** (adv.): in advance, beforehand.

15 **drug-damn'd**: damned for its use of poisons. **out-craftied**: outwitted.

16 **hard point**: crisis.

17 **of**: off. **extremity**: horror.

18 **mortal**: fatal.

20 **of**: by.

27 **breach**: violation of faith.

32 **pandar**: pimp, procurer,源自传说中特洛伊的拉皮条者 Pandarus,见莎剧 ***Troilus and Cressida***.

37 **worms**: serpents. **Nile**: 埃及的尼罗河,传说那里产毒蛇,见莎剧 ***Antony and Cleopatra***.

38 **posting**: speeding. **belie**: deceive.

39 **states**: statesmen.

40 **secrets**: unseen places, privacy.

41 **What cheer**: how is it with you.

Imo. False to his bed! What is it to be false?
To lie in watch there, and to think on him?
To weep 'twixt clock and clock? if sleep charge nature,
To break it with a fearful dream of him,
And cry myself awake? that 's false to bed, is it?

Pis. Alas, good lady!

Imo. I false! Thy conscience witness: Iachimo,
Thou didst accuse him of incontinency;
Thou then look'dst like a villain; now, methinks,
Thy favour 's good enough. Some jay of Italy,
Whose mother was her painting, hath betray'd him:
Poor I am stale, a garment out of fashion;
And, for I am richer than to hang by the walls,
I must be ripp'd:—to pieces with me! —O,
Men's vows are women's traitors! All good seeming
By thy revolt, O husband, shall be thought
Put on for villany; not born where 't grows,
But worn a bait for ladies.

Pis. Good madam, hear me.

Imo. True honest men being heard, like false Æneas,
Were in his time thought false; and Sinon's weeping
Did scandal many a holy tear, took pity
From most true wretchedness: so thou Posthumus,
Wilt lay the leaven on all proper men;
Goodly and gallant shall be false and perjured
From thy great fail. Come, fellow, be thou honest:
Do thou thy master's bidding. When thou see'st him,
A little witness my obedience. Look!
I draw the sword myself: take it, and hit
The innocent mansion of my love, my heart:
Fear not; 'tis empty of all things but grief:
Thy master is not there, who was indeed
The riches of it. Do his bidding; strike.
Thou mayst be valiant in a better cause,

43 **in watch**: awake. **on**: of.

44 **'twixt clock and clock**: hour by hour. **charge**: burden, overcome.

45 **of**: about.

51 **favour**: face, countenance. **jay**: strumpet.

52 **painting**: cosmetics.

53 **stale**: worse for age.

54 **for**: because. **richer than to**: too fine yet to.

55 **ripp'd**: cut up (for reuse).

56 **seeming**: appearance.

57 **revolt**: faithlessness, desertion.

60 **Æneas**, who deserted Dido,见 Virgil's ***Aeneid***.

61 **Sinon**, who betrayed the Trojans by persuading to admit the Trojan Horse.

62 **scandal**: discredit, make disreputable.

63 **From**: away from.

64 **lay the leaven on**: turn sour, corrupt. **leaven**: sour dough.

66 **fail**: failure.

68 **witness** (v. t.): testify to.

But now thou seem'st a coward.
Pis. Hence, vile instrument!
Thou shalt not damn my hand.
Imo. Why, I must die;
And if I do not by thy hand, thou art
No servant of thy master's. Against self-slaughter
There is a prohibition so divine
That cravens my weak hand. Come, here's my heart;—
Something 's afore 't. Soft, soft! We 'll no defence;—
Obedient as the scabbard. What is here?
The scriptures of the loyal Leonatus,
All turn'd to heresy? Away, away,
Corrupters of my faith! you shall no more
Be stomachers to my heart. Thus may poor fools
Believe false teachers: though those that are betray'd
Do feel the treason sharply, yet the traitor
Stands in worse case of woe.
And thou, Posthumus, thou that didst set up
My disobedience 'gainst the king my father,
And made me put into contempt the suits
Of princely fellows, shalt hereafter find
It is no act of common passage, but
A strain of rareness: and I grieve myself
To think, when thou shalt be disedged by her
That now thou tirest on, how thy memory
Will then be pang'd by me. Prithee, dispatch:
The lamb entreats the butcher: where 's thy knife?
Thou art too slow to do thy master's bidding,
When I desire it too.
Pis. O gracious lady,
Since I received command to do this business
I have not slept one wink.
Imo. Do 't, and to bed then.
Pis. I 'll wake mine eye-balls blind first.

79 prohibition,《圣经·出埃及记》第二十章摩西十诫中第六诫为“不可杀人”,此外《圣经》中对自杀并无明文禁令,但基督教会禁止自杀,自古已然。

80 cravens: makes cowardly.

81 afore 't: in front of it. **Soft**: hold, stop. **we'll** 后省略 have.

82 Obedient: as ready to receive the sword.

83 scriptures: holy writings, letters.

86 stomachers: 肚兜。

90 set up: instigate.

94 passage: occurrence.

96 disedged: taken off the edge of appetite, surfeited.

97 tirest on: seizes and feeds on ravenously (used of birds of prey).

98 dispatch: make haste.

103 to bed 前省略 go.

Imo. Wherefore then
Didst undertake it? Why hast thou abused
So many miles with a pretence? This place?
Mine action, and thine own? Our horses' labour?
The time inviting thee? the Perturb'd court,
For my being absent? Whereunto I never
Purpose return. Why hast thou gone so far,
To be unbent when thou hast ta'en thy stand,
The elected deer before thee?
Pis. But to win time
To lose so bad employment; in the which
I have consider'd of a course. Good lady,
Hear me with patience.
Imo. Talk thy tongue weary; speak:
I have heard I am a strumpet; and mine ear,
Therein false struck, can take no greater wound,
Nor tent to bottom that. But speak
Pis. Then, madam,
I thought you would not back again.
Imo. Most like,
Bringing me here to kill me.
Pis. Not so, neither:
But if I were as wise as honest, then
My purpose would prove well. It cannot be
But that my master is abused: some villain,
Ay, and singular in his art, hath done you both
This cursed injury.
Imo. Some Roman courtesan.
Pis. No, on my life.
I 'll give but notice you are dead, and send him
Some bloody sign of it; for 'tis commanded
I should do so: you shall be miss'd at court,
And that will well confirm it.
Imo. Why, good fellow,

105 **abused**：deceived.

108 **inviting**：calling on.

109 **whereunto**，i. e.，to the court.

110 **Purpose**：intend to.

111 **be unbent**：have you bow unbent. **stand**：shooting position.

112 **elected**：chosen.

113 **lose**：give up.

114 **consider'd of**：thought of.

118 **tent to bottom that**：probe that wound to its bottom. 医学上用探针探伤叫 tent.

119 **back** 前省略 go. **like**：likely.

123 **abused**：deceived.

124 **singular**：unmatched.

What shall I do the while? where abide? how live?
Or in my life what comfort, when I am
Dead to my husband?

Pis. If you 'll back to the court—

Imo. No court, no father; nor no more ado
With that harsh, noble, simple nothing,
That Cloten, whose love-suit hath been to me
As fearful as a siege.

Pis. If not at court,
Then not in Britain must you bide.

Imo. Where then?
Hath Britain all the sun that shines? Day, night,
Are they not but in Britain? I' the world's volume
Our Britain seems as of it, but not in 't;
In a great pool a swan's nest: prithee, think
There 's livers out of Britain.

Pis. I am most glad
You think of other place. The ambassador,
Lucius the Roman, comes to Milford-Haven
To-morrow: now, if you could wear a mind
Dark as your fortune is, and but disguise
That which, to appear itself, must not yet be
But by self-danger, you should tread a course
Pretty and full of view; yea, haply, near
The residence of Posthumus; so nigh at least
That though his actions were not visible, yet
Report should render him hourly to your ear
As truly as he moves.

Imo. O, for such means,
Though peril to my modesty, not death on 't,
I would adventure!

Pis. Well then, here 's the point:
You must forget to be a woman; change
Command into obedience; fear and niceness—

133 **back** 前省略 go.

135 **noble**：high-ranking. **simple**：foolish.

137 **fearful**：dreadful.

140 **Are they not but**：Do they exist only.

141 **of it**，i. e.，a page of the volume（book）. **in 't**，i. e.，bound into the volume.

143 **There's livers out of**：There are people living outside.

144 **other**：another or the other.

147 **Dark**：obscure.

148 **That**，i. e.，the fact that you are a woman. **to appear itself**：as regards showing itself.

149 **But by self-danger**：except to endanger yourself.

150 **Pretty**：pleasant. **view**：prospects.

153 **render**：describe.

156 **adventure**（v. i.）：venture，take the risk.

158 **Command**：the commanding ways of a princess. **niceness**：coyness.

The handmaids of all women, or, more truly,
Woman it pretty self—into a waggish courage;
Ready in gibes, quick-answer'd, saucy and
As quarrelous as the weasel; nay, you must
Forget that rarest treasure of your cheek,
Exposing it—but, O, the harder heart!
Alack, no remedy! —to the greedy touch
Of common-kissing Titan, and forget
Your laboursome and dainty trims, wherein
You made great Juno angry.

Imo. Nay, be brief:
I see into thy end, and am almost
A man already.

Pis. First, make yourself but like one.
Fore-thinking this, I have already fit—
'Tis in my cloak-bag—doublet, hat, hose, all
That answer to them: would you, in their serving
And with what imitation you can borrow
From youth of such a season, 'fore noble Lucius
Present yourself, desire his service, tell him
Wherein you 're happy,—which you 'll make him know,
If that his head have ear in music,—doubtless
With joy he will embrace you; for he 's honourable,
And, doubling that, most holy. Your means abroad,
You have me, rich; and I will never fail
Beginning nor supplyment.

Imo. Thou art all the comfort
The gods will diet me with. Prithee, away:
There 's more to be consider'd; but we 'll even
All that good time will give us: this attempt
I am soldier to, and will abide it with
A prince's courage. Away, I prithee.

Pis. Well, madam, we must take a short farewell,
Lest, being miss'd, I be suspected of

160 **Woman it pretty self**: pretty womanhood its self. **it**: its. **waggish**: roguish.

166 **common-kissing**: shining on everything alike. **Titan**, i. e., the Sun.

167 **laboursome**: elaborate. **trims**: ornamental dress.

168 **Juno**: 罗马神话中的天后。 **angry**: jealous.

169 **end**: purpose.

171 **Fore-thinking**: anticipating. **fit**: ready.

172 **doublet**: 男子紧身上衣。 **hose**: 男子紧身长裤。16—17 世纪英国服装。

173 **answer to**: go with. **in their serving**: with their help.

175 **season**: age. **'fore**: before.

176 **his service**: service under him.

177 **happy**: endowed, skillful. **make him know**: convince him.

178 **If that**: if.

180 **doubling that**: in addition. **means**: means of support.

182 **Beginning nor supplyment**: in providing the initial amount or in supplementing it.

183 **diet** (v. t.): feed.

184 **even** (v. t.): keep pace with.

186 **soldier to**: enlisted in, committed to. **abide**: face in fight, defy.

188 **short**: hasty.

Your carriage from the court. My noble mistress,
Here is a box; I had it from the queen:
What 's in 't is precious; if you are sick at sea,
Or stomach-qualm'd at land, a dram of this
Will drive away distemper. To some shade,
And fit you to your manhood: may the gods
Direct you to the best.

Imo. Amen: I thank thee. [*Exeunt severally.*

SCENE V

A room in Cymbeline's palace.

Enter Cymbeline, Queen, Cloten, Lucius, and Lords.

Cym. Thus far; and so farewell.

Luc. Thanks, royal sir.
My emperor hath wrote, I must from hence;
And am right sorry that I must report ye
My master's enemy.

Cym. Our subjects, sir,
Will not endure his yoke; and for ourself
To show less sovereignty than they, must needs
Appear unkinglike.

Luc. So, sir: I desire of you
A conduct over-land to Milford-Haven.
Madam, all joy befall your grace, and you!

Cym. My lords, you are appointed for that office;
The due of honour in no point omit.
So farewell, noble Lucius.

Luc. Your hand, my lord.

Clo. Receive it friendly; but from this time forth
I wear it as your enemy.

Luc. Sir, the event
Is yet to name the winner: fare you well.

190 **carriage**：removal.

193 **at land**：on land.

194 **distemper**：indisposition.

195 **fit**：dress. **to**：in accordance with.

197 **Amen**：基督教祈祷中的附和赞同语。

III. v.

2 **wrote**：written. **from** 前省略 go.

4 **Our** 和下行中的 **ourself** 都是用的 royal plural.

8 **conduct**：escort.

14 **wear it**：bear my hand. **event**：outcome.

Cym. Leave not the worthy Lucius, good my lords,
Till he have cross'd the Severn. Happiness!
[*Exeunt Lucius and Lords.*

Queen. He goes hence frowning: but it honours us
That we have given him cause.

Clo. 'Tis all the better;
Your valiant Britons have their wishes in it.

Cym. Lucius hath wrote already to the emperor
How it goes here. It fits us therefore ripely
Our chariots and our horsemen be in readiness:
The powers that he already hath in Gallia
Will soon be drawn to head, from whence he moves
His war for Britain.

Queen. 'Tis not sleepy business,
But must be look'd to speedily and strongly.

Cym. Our expectation that it would be thus
Hath made us forward. But, my gentle queen,
Where is our daughter? She hath not appear'd
Before the Roman, nor to us hath tender'd
The duty of the day: she looks us like
A thing more made of malice than of duty:
We have noted it. Call her before us, for
We have been too slight in sufferance.
[*Exit an Attendant.*

Queen. Royal sir,
Since the exile of Posthumus, most retired
Hath her life been; the cure whereof, my lord,
'Tis time must do. Beseech your majesty,
Forbear sharp speeches to her; she 's a lady
So tender of rebukes that words are strokes,
And strokes death to her.

Re-enter Attendant.

Cym. Where is she, sir? How

17 **the Severn**：英格兰和威尔士之间的界河。

21 **wrote**：written.

22 **fits**：befits. **ripely**：urgently.

24 **powers**：military forces. **he**，i. e.，the Roman emperor. **Gallia**：France.

25 **drawn to head**：assembled. **moves**：launches.

26 **sleepy**：lazy，inactive.

29 **forward**：well advanced in preparation.

32 **us**：to us.

35 **slight**：mild. **sufferance**：tolerance.

39 **Forbear**：refrain from.

40 **tender of**：sensitive to.

Can her contempt be answer'd?
Atten. Please you, sir,
Her chambers are all lock'd, and there 's no answer
That will be given to the loud'st of noise we make.
Queen. My lord, when last I went to visit her,
She pray'd me to excuse her keeping close;
Whereto constrain'd by her infirmity,
She should that duty leave unpaid to you,
Which daily she was bound to proffer: this
She wish'd me to make known; but our great court
Made me to blame in memory.
Cym. Her doors lock'd?
Not seen of late? Grant, heavens, that which I fear
Prove false! [*Exit.*
Queen. Son, I say, follow the king.
Clo. That man of hers, Pisanio, her old servant,
I have not seen these two days.
Queen. Go, look after.
[*Exit Cloten.*
Pisanio, thou that stand'st so for Posthumus!
He hath a drug of mine: I pray his absence
Proceed by swallowing that; for he believes
It is a thing most precious. But for her,
Where is she gone? Haply, despair hath seized her;
Or, wing'd with fervour of her love, she 's flown
To her desired Posthumus: gone she is
To death or to dishonour; and my end
Can make good use of either: she being down,
I have the placing of the British crown.

Re-enter Cloten.

How now, my son!
Clo. 'Tis certain she is fled.
Go in and cheer the king: he rages; none

46 **keeping close**: staying confined.

50 **court**: court business.

51 **to blame**: at fault.

56 **stand'st so for**: so much stand up for.

58 **Proceed by**: results from.

59 **for**: as for.

65 **placing**: disposal.

Dare come about him.
Queen. [*Aside*] All the better: may
This night forestall him of the coming day! [*Exit.*
Clo. I love and hate her: for she 's fair and royal,
And that she hath all courtly parts more exquisite
Than lady, ladies, woman; from every one
The best she hath, and she, of all compounded,
Outsells them all; I love her therefore: but
Disdaining me and throwing favours on
The low Posthumus slanders so her judgement
That what 's else rare is choked; and in that point
I will conclude to hate her, nay, indeed,
To be revenged upon her. For when fools
Shall—

Enter Pisanio.

Who is here? What, are you packing, sirrah?
Come hither: ah, you precious pandar! Villain,
Where is thy lady? In a word, or else
Thou art straightway with the fiends.
Pis. O, good my lord!
Clo. Where is thy lady? or, by Jupiter,—
I will not ask again. Close villain,
I 'll have this secret from thy heart, or rip
Thy heart to find it. Is she with Posthumus?
From whose so many weights of baseness cannot
A dram of worth be drawn.
Pis. Alas, my lord,
How can she be with him? When was she miss'd?
He is in Rome.
Clo. Where is she, sir? Come nearer;
No farther halting: satisfy me home
What is become of her.
Pis. O, my all-worthy lord!

69 **forestall**: deprive.

74 **Outsells**: exceeds in value.

76 **slanders**: discredits.

77 **else**: otherwise. **choked**: suffocated, made away with.

78 **conclude**: decide.

80 **packing**: going away.

85 **Close**: secretive.

88 **weights**: measures.

92 **satisfy me home**: fully tell me. **home** (adv.): completely.

Clo. All-worthy villain!
Discover where thy mistress is at once,
At the next word: no more of 'worthy lord!'
Speak, or thy silence on the instant is
Thy condemnation and thy death.
Pis. Then, sir,
This paper is the history of my knowledge
Touching her flight. [*Presenting a letter.*
Clo. Let 's see 't. I will pursue her
Even to Augustus' throne.
Pis. [*Aside*] Or this, or perish.
She 's far enough; and what he learns by this
May prove his travel, not her danger.
Clo. Hum!
Pis. [*Aside*] I 'll write to my lord she 's dead. O Imogen,
Safe mayst thou wander, safe return again!
Clo. Sirrah, is this letter true?
Pis. Sir, as I think.
Clo. It is Posthumus' hand; I know 't. Sirrah, if thou wouldst not be a villain, but do me true service, undergo those employments wherein I should have cause to use thee with a serious industry, that is, what villany soe'er I bid thee do, to perform it directly and truly, I would think thee an honest man: thou shouldst neither want my means for thy relief, nor my voice for thy preferment.
Pis. Well, my good lord.
Clo. Wilt thou serve me? For since patiently and constantly thou hast stuck to the bare fortune of that beggar Posthumus, thou canst not, in the course of gratitude, but be a diligent follower of mine. Wilt thou serve me?

95 Discover: reveal.

101 Or … or: either … or.

103 prove: turn out to mean.

110 undergo: undertake.

112 industry: diligence.

113 directly: promptly.

Pis. Sir, I will.

Clo. Give me thy hand; here 's my purse. Hast any of thy late master's garments in thy possession?

Pis. I have, my lord, at my lodging the same suit he wore when he took leave of my lady and mistress.

Clo. The first service thou dost me, fetch that suit hither: let it be thy first service; go.

Pis. I shall, my lord.

Clo. Meet thee at Milford-Haven! —I forgot to ask him one thing; I 'll remember 't anon:—even there, thou villain Posthumus, will I kill thee. I would these garments were come. She said upon a time—the bitterness of it I now belch from my heart—that she held the very garment of Posthumus in more respect than my noble and natural person, together with the adornment of my qualities. With that suit upon my back, will I ravish her: first kill him, and in her eyes; there shall she see my valour, which will then be a torment to her contempt. He on the ground, my speech of insultment ended on his dead body, and when my lust hath dined—which, as I say, to vex her I will execute in the clothes that she so praised—to the court I 'll knock her back, foot her home again. She hath despised me rejoicingly, and I 'll be merry in my revenge.

Re-enter Pisanio, with the clothes.

Be those the garments?

Pis. Ay, my noble lord.

Clo. How long is 't since she went to Milford-Haven?

Pis. She can scarce be there yet.

125 **late**: former.

138 **more respect**: higher regard.

141 **in her eyes**: within her sight.

144 **insultment**: contemptuous triumph.

148 **foot**: kick.

154 **scarce**: scarcely.

Clo. Bring this apparel to my chamber; that is the second thing that I have commanded thee: the third is, that thou wilt be a voluntary mute to my design. Be but duteous, and true preferment shall tender itself to thee . My revenge is now at Milford: would I had wings to follow it! Come, and be true. [*Exit.*

Pis. Thou bid'st me to my loss: for, true to thee
Were to prove false, which I will never be,
To him that is most true. To Milford go,
And find not her whom thou pursuest. Flow, flow,
You heavenly blessings, on her! This fool's speed
Be cross'd with slowness; labour be his meed!
[*Exit.*

SCENE VI

Wales: before the cave of Belarius.

Enter Imogen, in boy's clothes.

Imo. I see a man's life is a tedious one:
I have tired myself; and for two nights together
Have made the ground my bed. I should be sick,
But that my resolution helps me. Milford,
When from the mountain-top Pisanio show'd thee,
Thou wast within a ken: O Jove! I think
Foundations fly the wretched; such, I mean,
Where they should be relieved. Two beggars told me
I could not miss my way: will poor folks lie,
That have afflictions on them, knowing 'tis
A punishment or trial? Yes; no wonder,
When rich ones scarce tell true: to lapse in fulness
Is sorer than to lie for need; and falsehood
Is worse in kings than beggars. My dear lord!

157 **mute**: dumb spectator.

159 **tender**: offer, present.

162 **loss**: perdition.

167 **cross'd**: thwarted. **meed**: reward.

III. vi.

6 **within a ken**: within sight.

7 **Foundations**: charitable institutions.

10 **'tis**, i. e., poverty is.

11 **trial**: test of virtue.

12 **scarce**: scarcely. **true**: truth. **lapse**: sin, i. e., lie. **fulness**: affluence.

13 **sorer**: worse. **for**: on account of.

Thou art one o' the false ones: now I think on thee,
My hunger 's gone; but even before, I was
At point to sink for food. But what is this?
Here is a path to 't: 'tis some savage hold:
I were best not call; I dare not call; yet famine,
Ere clean it o'erthrow nature, makes it valiant.
Plenty and peace breeds cowards; hardness ever
Of hardiness is mother. Ho! who 's here!
If any thing that 's civil, speak; if savage,
Take or lend. Ho! No answer? then I 'll enter.
Best draw my sword; and if mine enemy
But fear the sword like me, he 'll scarcely look on 't.
Such a foe, good heavens! [*Exit, to the cave.*

Enter Belarius, Guiderius, and Arviragus.

Bel. You, Polydore, have proved best woodman and
Are master of the feast: Cadwal and I
Will play the cook and servant; 'tis our match:
The sweat of industry would dry and die,
But for the end it works to. Come; our stomachs
Will make what 's homely savoury: weariness
Can snore upon the flint, when resty sloth
Finds the down pillow hard. Now, peace be here,
Poor house, that keep'st thyself!

Gui. I am thoroughly weary.

Arv. I am weak with toil, yet strong in appetite.

Gui. There is cold meat i' the cave; we 'll browse on that,
Whilst what we have kill'd be cook'd.

Bel. [*Looking into the cave*] Stay; come not in.
But that it eats our victuals, I should think
Here were a fairy.

Gui. What 's the matter, sir?

Bel. By Jupiter, an angel! Or, if not,

16 **but even**: only a moment.

17 **At point to sink**: on the point of falling slowly to the ground. **for**: for lack of.

18 **hold**: fastness.

19 **were best**: had better.

20 **clean** (adv.): completely.

21 **Plenty and peace**,两个抽象名词视为单数。 **hardness**: hardship.

23 **civil**: civilized.

24 **Take or lend**: rob me or give me food.

25 **Best**: it is best for me to, I had better. **and if**: if.

27 **Such a foe** 前面省略 send me.

28 **woodman**: woodsman, hunter.

30 **match**: agreement.

31 **industry**: diligence.

34 **resty**: idle, torpid.

36 **keep'st thyself**: goes untended.

40 **But that**: except for the fact that. **victuals** ['vitlz]: food.

41 **were**,假设语气。

An earthly paragon! Behold divineness
No elder than a boy!

Re-enter Imogen.

Imo. Good masters, harm me not:
Before I enter'd here, I call'd; and thought
To have begg'd or bought what I have took: good troth,
I have stol'n nought: nor would not, though I had found
Gold strew'd i' the floor. Here 's money for my meat:
I would have left it on the board so soon
As I had made my meal, and parted
With prayers for the provider.
Gui. Money, youth?
Arv. All gold and silver rather turn to dirt!
As 'tis no better reckon'd, but of those
Who worship dirty gods.
Imo. I see you 're angry:
Know, if you kill me for my fault, I should
Have died had I not made it.
Bel. Whither bound?
Imo. To Milford-Haven.
Bel. What 's your name?
Imo. Fidele, sir. I have a kinsman who
Is bound for Italy; he embark'd at Milford;
To whom being going, almost spent with hunger,
I am fall'n in this offence.
Bel. Prithee, fair youth,
Think us no churls, nor measure our good minds
By this rude place we live in. Well encounter'd!
'Tis almost night: you shall have better cheer
Ere you depart: and thanks to stay and eat it.
Boys, bid him welcome.

44 **No elder**：not older.

46 **thought**：intended.

47 **took**：taken. **good troth**：in good truth，indeed.

49 **strew'd i'**：strewn on.

50 **so**：as.

54 **of**：by.

57 **made**：committed.

60 **Fidele**［fi'di:li，法、意］：faithful one.

62 **To whom being going**：to whom while I am going.

63 **in**：into.

66 **cheer**：food.

67 **Ere**：before. **to**：if you.

Gui. Were you a woman, youth,
I should woo hard but be your groom. In honesty,
I bid for you as I 'ld buy.
Arv. I 'll make 't my comfort
He is a man; I 'll love him as my brother:
And such a welcome as I 'ld give to him
After long absence, such is yours: most welcome!
Be sprightly, for you fall 'mongst friends.
Imo. 'Mongst friends,
If brothers. [*Aside*] Would it had been so, that they
Had been my father's sons! then had my prize
Been less, and so more equal ballasting
To thee, Posthumus.
Bel. He wrings at some distress.
Gui. Would I could free 't!
Arv. Or I; whate'er it be,
What pain it cost, what danger! Gods!
Bel. Hark, boys.
[*Whispering.*
Imo. Great men,
That had a court no bigger than this cave,
That did attend themselves and had the virtue
Which their own conscience seal'd them—laying by
That nothing-gift of differing multitudes—
Could not out-peer these twain. Pardon me, gods!
I 'ld change my sex to be companion with them,
Since Leonatus' false.
Bel. It shall be so.
Boys, we 'll go dress our hunt. Fair youth, come in:
Discourse is heavy, fasting; when we have supp'd,
We 'll mannerly demand thee of thy story,
So far as thou wilt speak it.
Gui. Pray, draw near.
Arv. The night to the owl and morn to the lark less

69 **but be**: rather than fail to be, if I could not be.

70 **buy**, i. e., marry you. **comfort**: joy, delight.

72 **him**, i. e., my brother.

74 **sprightly**: cheerful.

76 **had**: would be. **prize**: price, value.

77 **ballasting**: loading,船上载重压舱。这里说身份低些可与 Posthumus 更为匹配。

78 **wrings**: writhing in pain.

79 **free 't**: remove the distress.

83 **attend**: wait on. **virtue**: merit.

84 **conscience**: self-knowledge. **seal'd**: assured. **laying by**: disregarding.

85 **nothing-gift**: worthless gift, i. e., adulation. **differing**: (1) unable to agree on anything; (2) fickle.

86 **out-peer**: surpass.

89 **dress our hunt**: prepare the game killed for the table.

90 **Discourse** ... **fasting**: conversation is difficult when we are without food.

91 **demand**: inquire, ask. **of**: about, concerning.

welcome.

Imo. Thanks, sir.

Arv. I pray, draw near. [*Exeunt.*

SCENE VII

Rome. A public place.

Enter two Senators and Tribunes.

First Sen. This is the tenour of the emperor's writ:
That since the common men are now in action
'Gainst the Pannonians and Dalmatians,
And that the legions now in Gallia are
Full weak to undertake our wars against
The fall'n-off Britons, that we do incite
The gentry to this business. He creates
Lucius proconsul; and to you the tribunes,
For this immediate levy, he commends
His absolute commission. Long live Cæsar!

First Tri. Is Lucius general of the forces?

Sec. Sen. Ay.

First Tri. Remaining now in Gallia?

First Sen. With those legions
Which I have spoke of, whereunto your levy
Must be supplyant: the words of your commission
Will tie you to the numbers and the time
Of their dispatch.

First Tri. We will discharge our duty. [*Exeunt.*

III. vii.

5 **Full weak**：too weak.

6 **fall'n-off**：revolted.

8 **proconsul**：古罗马一个省的督军。

9 **commends**：entrusts.

10 **commission**：authorization to act.

13 **spoke**：spoken.

14 **supplyant**：auxiliary.

15 **tie**：bind.

ACT IV

SCENE I

Wales: near the cave of Belarius.

Enter Cloten alone.

Clo. I am near to the place where they should meet, if Pisanio have mapped it truly. How fit his garments serve me! Why should his mistress, who was made by him that made the tailor, not be fit too? the rather—saving reverence of the word—for 'tis said a woman's fitness comes by fits. Therein I must play the workman. I dare speak it to myself—for it is not vain-glory for a man and his glass to confer in his own chamber—I mean, the lines of my body are as well drawn as his; no less young, more strong, not beneath him in fortunes, beyond him in the advantage of the time, above him in birth, alike conversant in general services, and more remarkable in single oppositions: yet this imperceiverant thing loves him in my despite. What mortality is! Posthumus, thy head, which now is growing upon thy shoulders, shall within this hour be off; thy mistress enforced; thy garments cut to pieces before thy face: and all this done, spurn her home to her father; who may haply be a little angry for my so rough usage; but my mother, having power of his testiness, shall turn all into my commendations. My

IV. i.

2 **fit**: aptly. **his**, i. e., Posthumus's.

4 **him**, i. e., God.

5—6 **saving reverence of the word**: God protecting your reverence from the word; pardon the expression.

6 **fitness**: sexual inclination.

9 **glass**: mirror.

14 **conversant**: versed, knowledgeable. **general services**: war duties.

15 **single oppositions**: single combats, duels.

15—16 **imperceiverant**: imperseverant, thoughtless.

16 **What** 之后省略 a thing.

17 **mortality**: human life; mankind.

19 **enforced**: raped.

22 **haply**: perhaps.

23 **power of**: control over.

horse is tied up safe: out, sword, and to a sore purpose! Fortune, put them into my hand! This is the very description of their meeting-place; and the fellow dares not deceive me. [*Exit.*

SCENE II

Before the cave of Belarius.

Enter, from the cave, Belarius, Guiderius, Arviragus, and Imogen.

Bel. [*To Imogen*] You are not well: remain here in the cave;
We 'll come to you after hunting.
Arv. [*To Imogen*] Brother, stay here:
Are we not brothers?
Imo. So man and man should be;
But clay and clay differs in dignity,
Whose dust is both alike. I am very sick.
Gui. Go you to hunting; I 'll abide with him.
Imo. So sick I am not, yet I am not well;
But not so citizen a wanton as
To seem to die ere sick: so please you, leave me;
Stick to your journal course: the breach of custom
Is breach of all. I am ill, but your being by me
Cannot amend me: society is no comfort
To one not sociable; I am not very sick,
Since I can reason of it. Pray you, trust me here:
I 'll rob none but myself; and let me die,
Stealing so poorly.
Gui. I love thee; I have spoke it:
How much the quantity, the weight as much,
As I do love my father.
Bel. What! how! how!

25 **sore**：grievous.

IV. ii.

4 **clay and clay**：different persons.《圣经》上说上帝用土造人，故以土代人。 **dignity**：social position.

5 **dust**，人死均归于尘土。

6 **abide**：stay.

8 **citizen**（adj.）：city-bred，effeminate. **wanton**：one brought up in luxury.

10 **journal course**：daily routine.

12 **amend**：make better.

14 **reason of**：talk sensibly about.

16 **so poorly**：one so poor as myself. **spoke**：spoken，said.

17 **How much the quantity**：as greatly.

Arv. If it be sin to say so, sir, I yoke me
In my good brother's fault: I know not why
I love this youth; and I have heard you say,
Love's reason 's without reason: the bier at door
And a demand who is 't shall die, I 'ld say
'My father, not this youth.'
Bel. [*Aside*] O noble strain!
O worthiness of nature! breed of greatness!
Cowards father cowards and base things sire base:
Nature hath meal and bran, contempt and grace.
I 'm not their father; yet who this should be,
Doth miracle itself, loved before me. —
'Tis the ninth hour o' the morn.
Arv. Brother, farewell.
Imo. I wish ye sport.
Arv. You health. So please you, sir.
Imo. [*Aside*] These are kind creatures. Gods, what lies I have heard!
Our courtiers say all 's savage but at court:
Experience, O, thou disprovest report!
The imperious seas breed monsters; for the dish
Poor tributary rivers as sweet fish.
I am sick still, heart-sick. Pisanio,
I 'll now taste of thy drug. [*Swallows some.*
Gui. I could not stir him:
He said he was gentle, but unfortunate;
Dishonestly afflicted, but yet honest.
Arv. Thus did he answer me: yet said, hereafter
I might know more.
Bel. To the field, to the field!
We 'll leave you for this time: go in and rest.
Arv. We 'll not be long away.
Bel. Pray, be not sick,
For you must be our housewife.

19 **yoke me**: share.

22 **bier**: litter for carrying a corpse.

24 **strain**: inherited character.

27 **meal and bran**: flour and husks.

29 **miracle itself**: make itself a miracle. **before**: more than.

31 **sport**: pastime, pleasure.

33 **but**: except.

35 **imperious**: imperial, high.

38 **stir him**: make him tell his story.

39 **gentle**: of noble birth.

Imo. Well or ill,
I am bound to you.
Bel. And shalt be ever.
[*Exit Imogen, to the cave.*
This youth, howe'er distress'd, appears he hath had
Good ancestors.
Arv. How angel-like he sings!
Gui. But his neat cookery! he cut our roots
In characters;
And sauced our broths, as Juno had been sick,
And he her dieter.
Arv. Nobly he yokes
A smiling with a sigh, as if the sigh
Was that it was, for not being such a smile;
The smile mocking the sigh, that it would fly
From so divine a temple, to commix
With winds that sailors rail at.
Gui. I do note
That grief and patience, rooted in him both,
Mingle their spurs together.
Arv. Grow, patience!
And let the stinking elder, grief, untwine
His perishing root with the increasing vine!
Bel. It is great morning. Come, away! —Who 's there?

Enter Cloten.

Clo. I cannot find those runagates; that villain
Hath mock'd me: I am faint.
Bel. 'Those runagates!'
Means he not us? I partly know him; 'tis
Cloten, the son o' the queen. I fear some ambush.
I saw him not these many years, and yet
I know 'tis he. We are held as outlaws: hence!
Gui. He is but one: you and my brother search

46 bound：(1) indebted；(2) tied by affection.

47 he hath：to have.

50 as：as if.

51 dieter：cook.

53 that：what.

54 that：because.

55 commix：join.

58 spurs：roots.

59 elder：接骨木，其叶和花有臭味。传说背叛耶稣的犹大系在一株接骨木树上吊死。

60 His：its. **perishing**：destructive. **with**：from. **vine**，指 patience.

61 great morning：full daylight.

62 runagates：runaways，i. e.，Posthumus and Imogen. **villain**，i. e.，Pisanio.

63 mock'd：deceived.

67 held：regarded.

What companies are near: pray you, away;
Let me alone with him.
[*Exeunt Belarius and Arviragus.*

Clo. Soft! What are you
That fly me thus? some villain mountaineers?
I have heard of such. What slave art thou?

Gui. A thing
More slavish did I ne'er than answering
A slave without a knock.

Clo. Thou art a robber,
A law-breaker, a villain: yield thee, thief.

Gui. To who? to thee? What art thou? Have not I
An arm as big as thine? a heart as big?
Thy words, I grant, are bigger; for I wear not
My dagger in my mouth. Say what thou art,
Why I should yield to thee.

Clo. Thou villain base,
Know'st me not by my clothes?

Gui. No, nor thy tailor, rascal,
Who is thy grandfather: he made those clothes,
Which, as it seems, make thee.

Clo. Thou precious varlet,
My tailor made them not.

Gui. Hence then, and thank
The man that gave them thee. Thou art some fool;
I am loath to beat thee.

Clo. Thou injurious thief,
Hear but my name, and tremble.

Gui. What 's thy name?

Clo. Cloten, thou villain.

Gui. Cloten, thou double villain, be thy name,
I cannot tremble at it: were it Toad, or Adder, Spider,
'Twould move me sooner.

Clo. To thy further fear,

69 companies: companions.

70 Let: leave. **Soft**: hold, stop.

71 fly: flee from.

74 without a knock: without knocking him down.

76 To who: to whom.

83 precious: of great value, here used ironically. **varlet**: knave, rascal.

86 injurious: insulting.

Nay, to thy mere confusion, thou shalt know
I am son to the queen.

Gui. I am sorry for 't: not seeming
So worthy as thy birth.

Clo. Art not afeard?

Gui. Those that I reverence, those I fear, the wise:
At fools I laugh, not fear them.

Clo. Die the death:
When I have slain thee with my proper hand,
I 'll follow those that even now fled hence,
And on the gates of Lud's town set your heads:
Yield, rustic mountaineer. [*Exeunt, fighting.*

Re-enter Belarius and Arviragus.

Bel. No companies abroad?

Arv. None in the world: you did mistake him, sure.

Bel. I cannot tell: long is it since I saw him,
But time hath nothing blurr'd those lines of favour
Which then he wore; the snatches in his voice,
And burst of speaking, were as his: I am absolute
'Twas very Cloten.

Arv. In this place we left them:
I wish my brother make good time with him,
You say he is so fell.

Bel. Being scarce made up,
I mean, to man, he had not apprehension
Of roaring terrors: for defect of judgement
Is oft the cause of fear. But see, thy brother.

Re-enter Guiderius, with Cloten's head.

Gui. This Cloten was a fool, an empty purse;
There was no money in 't: not Hercules
Could have knocked out his brains, for he had none:
Yet I not doing this, the fool had borne

92 **mere**：unqualified，absolute. **confusion**：ruin.

94 **So worthy as**：worthy of，as worthy as.

95 **reverence**（v. t.）：regard with veneration. **fear**：hold in awe.

97 **proper**：own.

99 **Lud's town**：London. 见 III. i. 3. 旧时在伦敦桥或其他公共场所悬挂犯人头示众。

101 **abroad**：about.

104 **favour**：face. **lines of favour**：facial features.

105 **snatches**：catches，hesitations.

107 **very Cloten**：Cloten himself.

108 **make good time with**：do well against，is successful with.

109 **fell**：fierce，aggressive. **scarce made up**：scarcely grown-up.

114 **Hercules**：希腊传说中的大力士。

116 **Yet I not doing this**：if I had not done this. **had borne**：would have won（carried away）.

My head as I do his.

Bel. What hast thou done?

Gui. I am perfect what: cut off one Cloten's head,
Son to the queen, after his own report;
Who call'd me traitor, mountaineer; and swore,
With his own single hand he 'ld take us in,
Displace our heads where—thank the gods! —They grow.
And set them on Lud's town.

Bel. We are all undone.

Gui. Why, worthy father, what have we to lose,
But that he swore to take, our lives? The law
Protects not us: then why should we be tender
To let an arrogant piece of flesh threat us,
Play judge and executioner, all himself,
For we do fear the law? What company
Discover you abroad?

Bel. No single soul
Can we set eye on; but in all safe reason
He must have some attendants. Though his humour
Was nothing but mutation, ay, and that
From one bad thing to worse, not frenzy, not
Absolute madness could so far have raved,
To bring him here alone: although perhaps
It may be heard at court that such as we
Cave here, hunt here, are outlaws, and in time
May make some stronger head; the which he hearing—
As it is like him—might break out, and swear
He 'ld fetch us in; yet is 't not probable
To come alone, either he so undertaking,
Or they so suffering: then on good ground we fear,
If we do fear this body hath a tail
More perilous than the head.

Arv. Let ordinance

118 **perfect**: certain.

119 **after**: according to.

121 **take us in**: capture us.

122 **where**: from where.

125 **But that**: except what.

126 **tender**: meek, gentle.

129 **For**: because.

131 **safe**: sound.

132 **humour**: disposition.

133 **mutation**: changeableness.

135 **raved**: been delirious, acted like a madman.

138 **Cave** (v. i.): live in a cave.

139 **make … head**: raise … an armed force.

143 **suffering**: allowing.

144 **tail**: follow-up force.

145 **ordinance**: what is ordained, destiny.

Come as the gods foresay it: howsoe'er,
My brother hath done well.
Bel. I had no mind
To hunt this day: the boy Fidele's sickness
Did make my way long forth.
Gui. With his own sword,
Which he did wave against my throat, I have ta'en
His head from him: I ll throw 't into the creek
Behind our rock, and let it to the sea,
And tell the fishes he 's the queen's son, Cloten:
That 's all I reck. [*Exit.*
Bel. I fear 'twill be revenged:
Would, Polydore, thou hadst not done 't! Though valour
Becomes thee well enough.
Arv. Would I had done 't,
So the revenge alone pursued me! Polydore,
I love thee brotherly, but envy much
Thou hast robb'd me of this deed: I would revenges,
That possible strength might meet, would seek us through
And put us to our answer.
Bel. Well, 'tis done:
We 'll hunt no more to-day, nor seek for danger
Where there 's no profit. I prithee, to our rock;
You and Fidele play the cooks: I 'll stay
Till hasty Polydore return, and bring him
To dinner presently.
Arv. Poor sick Fidele!
I 'll willingly to him: to gain his colour
I 'ld let a parish of such Clotens blood,
And praise myself for charity. [*Exit.*
Bel. O thou goddess,
Thou divine Nature, how thyself thou blazon'st
In these two princely boys! They are as gentle

146 foresay：predict. **howsoe'er**：howsoever it be，in any case.

149 my way long forth：my journey forth long (tedious).

152 to 前省略 go.

154 reck：care.

155 Would：I wish.

157 So：so that. **alone** 的位置应在 me 后。

159 robb'd：deprived.

160 possible：all our potential. **through**：out.

161 put us to our answer：force us to retaliate.

165 hasty：rash.

167 to him 前省略 go. **gain**：restore.

168 parish of such Clotens blood：blood of a whole church-district of such people like Cloten.

170 blazon'st：proclaim or display (as in a blazon or coat of arms).

As zephyrs blowing below the violet,
Not wagging his sweet head; and yet as rough,
Their royal blood enchafed, as the rudest wind
That by the top doth take the mountain pine
And make him stoop to the vale. 'Tis wonder
That an invisible instinct should frame them
To royalty unlearn'd, honour untaught,
Civility not seen from other, valour
That wildly grows in them, but yields a crop
As if it had been sow'd. Yet still it 's strange
What Cloten's being here to us portends,
Or what his death will bring us.

Re-enter Guiderius.

Gui. Where 's my brother?
I have sent Cloten's clotpoll down the stream,
In embassy to his mother: his body's hostage
For his return. [*Solemn music.*

Bel. My ingenious instrument!
Hark, Polydore, it sounds! But what occasion
Hath Cadwal now to give it motion? Hark!

Gui. Is he at home?

Bel. He went hence even now.

Gui. What does he mean? Since death of my dear'st mother
It did not speak before. All solemn things
Should answer solemn accidents. The matter?
Triumphs for nothing and lamenting toys
Is jollity for apes and grief for boys.
Is Cadwal mad?

Re-enter Arviragus with Imogen, as dead, bearing her in his arms.

Bel. Look, here he comes,

172 **zephyrs** [ˈzefəs]：希腊神话中的西风，系温和的微风。

174 **enchafed**：enflamed，heated in anger.

177 **frame**：shape.

179 **other**：others.

180 **wildly**：naturally，spontaneously.

184 **clotpoll**：blockhead，head.

185 **his body's**：Cloten's body is.

186 **his**：its，i. e.，his head's.

188 **motion**：tuning.

190 **death** 前省略 the.

192 **answer**：be in response to. **accidents**：events. **The matter**：what is the matter.

193 **toys**：trifles.

And brings the dire occasion in his arms
Of what we blame him for!
Arv. The bird is dead
That we have made so much on. I had rather
Have skipp'd from sixteen years of age to sixty,
To have turn'd my leaping-time into a crutch,
Than have seen this.
Gui. O sweetest, fairest lily!
My brother wears thee not the one half so well
As when thou grew'st thyself.
Bel. O melancholy!
Who ever yet could sound thy bottom? Find
The ooze, to show what coast thy sluggish crare
Might easiliest harbour in? Thou blessed thing!
Jove knows what man thou mightst have made; but I,
Thou diedst, a most rare boy, of melancholy.
How found you him?
Arv. Stark, as you see:
Thus smiling, as some fly had tickled slumber
Not as death's dart, being laugh'd at; his right cheek
Reposing on a cushion.
Gui. Where?
Arv. O' the floor;
His arms thus leagued: I thought he slept, and put
My clouted brogues from off my feet, whose rudeness
Answer'd my steps too loud.
Gui. Why, he but sleeps:
If he be gone, he 'll make his grave a bed;
With female fairies will his tomb be haunted,
And worms will not come to thee.
Arv. With fairest flowers,
Whilst summer lasts, and I live here, Fidele,
I 'll sweeten thy sad grave: thou shalt not lack
The flower that 's like thy face, pale primrose, nor

196 **occasion**：cause，接下行 of 短语。

198 **on**：of.

200 **leaping-time**：time of swift motion，youth. **crutch**：拐杖，i. e.，old age.

204 **sound thy bottom**：sound your（melancholy's）depth.

205 **sluggish**：slow. **crare**：trading vessel.

207 **what** 后省略 a. **I** 后省略 know.

209 **Stark**：stiff.

210 **as**：as if.

213 **leagued**：folded together.

214 **clouted brogues**：hobnailed boots.

215 **Answer'd**：resounded. **but**：only.

220 **sweeten**：make fragrant.

221 **primrose**：报春花。

The azured harebell, like thy veins; no, nor
The leaf of eglantine, whom not to slander,
Out-sweeten'd not thy breath: the ruddock would
With charitable bill—O bill, sore shaming
Those rich-left heirs that let their fathers lie
Without a monument! —bring thee all this;
Yea, and furr'd moss besides, when flowers are none,
To winter-ground thy corse.

Gui. Prithee, have done;
And do not play in wench-like words with that
Which is so serious. Let us bury him,
And not protract with admiration what
Is now due debt. To the grave!

Arv. Say, where shall's lay him?

Gui. By good Euriphile, our mother.

Arv. Be 't so:
And let us, Polydore, though now our voices
Have got the mannish crack, sing him to the ground,
As once our mother; use like note and words,
Save that 'Euriphile' must be 'Fidele.'

Gui. Cadwal,
I cannot sing: I 'll weep, and word it with thee:
For notes of sorrow out of tune are worse
Than priests and fanes that lie.

Arv. We 'll speak it then.

Bel. Great griefs, I see, medicine the less; for Cloten
Is quite forgot. He was a queen's son, boys:
And though he came our enemy, remember
He was paid for that: though mean and mighty, rotting
Together, have one dust, yet reverence,
That angel of the world, doth make distinction
Of place 'tween high and low. Our foe was princely;
And though you took his life as being our foe,
Yet bury him as a prince.

222 harebell：风铃草(浅蓝色花)。

223 eglantine：香叶蔷薇。 **whom not to slander**：which，not to depreciate it.

224 Out-sweeten'd not：would not out-sweeten. **ruddock**：robin redbreast，红胸知更鸟，传说它喜叼花叶到墓上铺盖。

225 sore (adv.)：sorely，grievously.

230 winter-ground (v. t.)：inter during winter. **corse**：corpse.

231 wench-like：woman-like，womanish.

233 admiration：wonder.

234 shall's：shall we.

238 As once 后省略 we sang. **note**：tune.

240 word (v. t.)：speak.

242 fanes：temples.

243 medicine (v. i.)：curse.

244 forgot：forgotten.

246 paid：punished.

248 angel of the world：messenger from heaven to the earth. 旧时基督教认为地上的等级制是天上的等级制 hierarchy 的模拟物，尊重高贵等级即为 reverence.

Gui. Pray you, fetch him hither,
Thersites' body is as good as Ajax',
When neither are alive.
Arv. If you 'll go fetch him,
We 'll say our song the whilst. Brother, begin.
[*Exit Belarius.*
Gui. Nay, Cadwal, we must lay his head to the east;
My father hath a reason for 't.
Arv. 'Tis true.
Gui. Come on then and remove him.
Arv. So. Begin.

SONG.

Gui. Fear no more the heat o' the sun,
Nor the furious winter's rages;
Thou thy worldly task hast done,
Home art gone and ta'en thy wages:
Golden lads and girls all must,
As chimney-sweepers, come to dust.

Arv. Fear no more the frown o' the great;
Thou art past the tyrant's stroke;
Care no more to clothe and eat;
To thee the reed is as the oak:
The sceptre, learning, physic, must
All follow this and come to dust.

Gui. Fear no more the lightning-flash,
Arv. Nor the all-dreaded thunder-stone;
Gui. Fear not slander, censure rash;
Arv. Thou hast finish'd joy and moan:
Both. All lovers young, all lovers must
Consign to thee and come to dust.

Gui. No exorciser harm thee!
Arv. Nor no witchcraft charm thee!

252 特洛伊战争时，Thersites 是希腊营中最下贱胆怯的兵士，而 Ajax 则是高贵英勇的大将。

253 **neither** 视为复数。

254 **the whilst**：in the meantime.

255 **to**：toward. 葬尸头朝东是凯尔特人非基督教的习俗。

261 **Home art gone**：have gone home.

263 **As**：like；267 行同。

265 **past**：beyond.

268 **physic**：medical knowledge.

271 **thunder-stone**：thunderbolt.

275 **Consign to**：submit to the same terms as.

276 **exorciser**：raiser of spirits.

Gui. Ghost unlaid forbear thee!
Arv. Nothing ill come near thee!
Both. Quiet consummation have;
And renowned be thy grave!

Re-enter Belarius with the body of Cloten.

Gui. We have done our obsequies: come lay him down.
Bel. Here 's a few flowers, but 'bout midnight more:
The herbs that have on them cold dew o' the night
Are strewings fitt'st for graves. Upon their faces.
You were as flowers, now wither'd: even so
These herblets shall, which we upon you strow.
Come on, away: apart upon our knees.
The ground that gave them first has them again:
Their pleasures here are past, so is their pain.
[*Exeunt Belarius, Guiderius, and Arviragus.*
Imo. [*Awaking*] Yes, sir, to Milford-Haven; which is the way? —
I thank you. —By yond bush? —Pray, how far thither?
'Ods pittikins! can it be six mile yet? —
I have gone all night: faith, I 'll lie down and sleep.
But, soft! no bedfellow! O gods and goddesses!
[*Seeing the body of Cloten.*
These flowers are like the pleasures of the world;
This bloody man, the care on 't. I hope I dream;
For so I thought I was a cave-keeper,
And cook to honest creatures: but 'tis not so;
'Twas but a bolt of nothing, shot at nothing,
Which the brain makes of fumes: our very eyes
Are sometimes like our judgements, blind. Good faith,
I tremble still with fear: but if there be
Yet left in heaven as small a drop of pity
As a wren's eye, fear'd gods, a part of it!

278 **unlaid**：not laid to rest. **forbear thee**：leave you alone.

280 **consummation**：ending.

283 **a few** 视为单数。

285 **Upon their faces**，此三字，连其前后标点和首字母大写全有疑问，考证者诸多猜测，均无定论。

287 **shall**，i. e.，shall wither. **strow**：strew.

288 **apart**：elsewhere.

289 **gave them**，i. e.，gave them life.

293 **'Ods pittikins**：By God's pity，a mild oath.

294 **gone**：walked.

295 **soft**：hold，wait.

297 **care on 't**：sorrow of the world.

298 **For so**：for then. **cave-keeper**：cave-dweller.

300 **bolt**：arrow.

301 **fumes**：vapours，旧时认为胃产生气，使脑迷惑做梦。

305 **wren**：鹪鹩，一种很小的鸟。

The dream 's here still: even when I wake, it is
Without me, as within me: not imagined, felt.
A headless man! The garments of Posthumus!
I know the shape of's leg: this is his hand;
His foot Mercurial; his Martial thigh;
The brawns of Hercules: but his Jovial face—
Murder in heaven? —How! —'Tis gone. Pisanio,
All curses madded Hecuba gave the Greeks,
And mine to boot, be darted on thee! Thou,
Conspired with that irregulous devil, Cloten,
Hast here cut off my lord. To write and read
Be henceforth treacherous! Damn'd Pisanio
Hath with his forged letters—damn'd Pisanio—
From this most bravest vessel of the world
Struck the main-top! O Posthumus! alas,
Where is thy head? where 's that? Ay me! where 's that?
Pisanio might have kill'd thee at the heart
And left this head on. How should this be? Pisanio?
'Tis he and Cloten: malice and lucre in them
Have laid this woe here. O, 'tis pregnant, pregnant!
The drug he gave me, which he said was precious
And cordial to me, have I not found it
Murderous to the senses? That confirms it home:
This is Pisanio's deed, and Cloten's: O!
Give colour to my pale cheek with thy blood,
That we the horrider may seem to those
Which chance to find us: O, my lord, my lord!
[*Falls on the body.*

Enter Lucius, a Captain and other Officers, and a Soothsayer.

Cap. To them the legions garrison'd in Gallia
After your will have cross'd the sea, attending

310 **Mercurial**：like Mercury's；罗马神话中的神的使者 Mercury，走路极快。 **Martial**：like Mars's；罗马神话中的战神 Mars，腿粗壮有力。

311 **brawns**：muscles. **Jovial**：like Jove's.

312 **'Tis**：his face (head) is.

313 **All curses**：may all the curses that … 下接 be darted on thee. **madded**：maddened. **Hecuba**：Troy 王后，因家破城亡而疯狂，思复仇而咒骂希腊人。

314 **to boot**：into the bargain. **darted on**：shot at，directed at.

315 **Conspired**：conspiring. **irregulous**：lawless.

319 **most bravest**：finest，双料最高级。

320 **main-top**：top of the mast.

324 **lucre**：greed.

325 **laid**：contrived. **pregnant**：most probable，evident.

327 **cordial**：restorative，strengthening the heart.

328 **home** (adv.)：to the full.

331 **That**：so that. **horrider**：more terrifying.

333 **To**：in addition to.

334 **After your will**：according to your command. **attending**：waiting for.

You here at Milford-Haven with your ships:
They are in readiness.
Luc. But what from Rome?
Cap. The senate hath stirr'd up the confiners
And gentlemen of Italy, most willing spirits
That promise noble service: and they come
Under the conduct of bold Iachimo,
Syenna's brother.
Luc. When expect you them?
Cap. With the next benefit o' the wind.
Luc. This forwardness
Makes our hopes fair. Command our present numbers
Be muster'd; bid the captains look to 't. Now, sir,
What have you dream'd of late of this war's purpose?
Sooth. Last night the very gods show'd me a vision—
I fast and pray'd for their intelligence—thus:
I saw Jove's bird, the Roman eagle, wing'd
From the spongy south to this part of the west,
There vanish'd in the sunbeams: which portends—
Unless my sins abuse my divination—
Success to the Roman host.
Luc. Dream often so,
And never false. Soft, ho! what trunk is here
Without his top? The ruin speaks that sometime
It was a worthy building. How! a page!
Or dead, or sleeping on him? But dead rather;
For nature doth abhor to make his bed
With the defunct, or sleep upon the dead.
Let's see the boys face.
Cap. He 's alive, my lord.
Luc. He 'll then instruct us of this body. Young one,
Inform us of thy fortunes, for it seems
They crave to be demanded. Who is this
Thou makest thy bloody pillow? Or who was he

337 **confiners**：inhabitants.

338 **spirits**：persons.

340 **conduct**：command.

341 **Syenna**：Duke of Siena（意大利西中部城市）。

342 **forwardness**：readiness.

343 **numbers**：soldiers.

345 **purpose**：outcome.

347 **fast**：fasted；尾音为 t，省略 ed. **intelligence**：information.

348 **wing'd**：flew.

349 **spongy**：damp.

351 **abuse**：falsify.

353 **false**（adv.）：falsely.

354 **his**：its. **top**：head. **sometime**：once.

356 **Or**：either.

360 **instruct us of**：inform us about.

That, otherwise than noble nature did,
Hath alter'd that good picture? What 's thy interest
In this sad wreck? How came it? Who is it?
What art thou?

Imo. I am nothing: or if not,
Nothing to be were better. This was my master,
A very valiant Briton and a good,
That here by mountaineers lies slain. Alas!
There is no more such masters: I may wander
From east to occident, cry out for service,
Try many, all good, serve truly, never
Find such another master.

Luc. 'Lack, good youth!
Thou movest no less with thy complaining than
Thy master in bleeding: say his name, good friend.

Imo. Richard du Champ. [*Aside*] If I do lie, and do
No harm by it, though the gods hear, I hope
They 'll pardon it. Say you, sir?

Luc. Thy name?

Imo. Fidele, sir.

Luc. Thou dost approve thyself the very same:
Thy name well fits thy faith, thy faith thy name.
Wilt take thy chance with me? I will not say
Thou shalt be so well master'd, but be sure,
No less beloved. The Roman emperor's letters
Sent by a consul to me should not sooner
Than thine own worth prefer thee: go with me.

Imo. I 'll follow, sir. But first, an 't please the gods,
I 'll hide my master from the flies, as deep
As these poor pickaxes can dig: and when
With wild wood-leaves and weeds I ha' strew'd his grave
And on it said a century of prayers,
Such as I can, twice o'er, I 'll weep and sigh,

364 **otherwise … did**：acting differently than nature.

368 **Nothing … better**：it were better to be nothing.

371 **masters** 多数，仍用 there is 单数动词。

374 **'Lack**：alack，alas.

380 **approve**：prove，show.

386 **prefer**：recommend. 下 400 行同。

387 **an 't**：if it.

389 **pickaxes**，i. e.，hands.

391 **century**：hundred.

And leaving so his service, follow you,
So please you entertain me.

Luc. Ay, good youth;
And rather father thee than master thee.
My friends,
The boy hath taught us manly duties: let us
Find out the prettiest daisied plot we can,
And make him with our pikes and partisans
A grave: come, arm him. Boy, he is preferr'd
By thee to us, and he shall be interr'd
As soldiers can. Be cheerful; wipe thine eyes:
Some falls are means the happier to arise. [*Exeunt.*

SCENE III

A room in Cymbeline's palace.

Enter Cymbeline, Lords, Pisanio, and Attendants.

Cym. Again; and bring me word how 'tis with her.
[*Exit an Attendant.*
A fever with the absence of her son;
A madness, of which her life 's in danger. Heavens,
How deeply you at once do touch me! Imogen,
The great part of my comfort, gone; my queen
Upon a desperate bed, and in a time
When fearful wars point at me; her son gone,
So needful for this present: it strikes me, past
The hope of comfort. But for thee, fellow,
Who needs must know of her departure and
Dost seem so ignorant, we 'll enforce it from thee
By a sharp torture.

Pis. Sir, my life is yours,
I humbly set it at your will: but, for my mistress,
I nothing know where she remains, why gone,

394 entertain：employ.

398 daisied：grown with daisies.

399 pikes：spears. **partisans**：古罗马人用的长柄斧。

400 arm (v. t.)：lift.

403 means the happier to arise：means by which good fortune arises.

IV. iii.

1 her，指续娶的王后，Cloten 之母。

2 with：on account of.

4 touch：afflict.

8 needful：needed.

9 for：as for.

11 enforce：obtain by force.

12 sharp：harsh，severe.

13 for：as for. 下第 19 行同。

Nor when she purposes return. Beseech your highness,
Hold me your loyal servant.
First Lord. Good my liege,
The day that she was missing he was here:
I dare be bound he 's true and shall perform
All parts of his subjection loyally. For Cloten,
There wants no diligence in seeking him,
And will, no doubt, be found.
Cym. The time is troublesome.
[*To Pisanio*] We 'll slip you for a season; but our jealousy
Does yet depend.
First Lord. So please your majesty,
The Roman legions, all from Gallia drawn,
Are landed on your coast, with a supply
Of Roman gentlemen by the senate sent.
Cym. Now for the counsel of my son and queen!
I am amazed with matter.
First Lord. Good my liege,
Your preparation can affront no less
Than what you hear of: come more, for more you 're ready:
The want is but to put those powers in motion
That long to move.
Cym. I thank you. Let's withdraw;
And meet the time as it seeks us. We fear not
What can from Italy annoy us, but
We grieve at chances here. Away!
[*Exeunt all but Pisanio.*
Pis. I heard no letter from my master since
I wrote him Imogen was slain: 'tis strange:
Nor hear I from my mistress, who did promise
To yield me often tidings; neither know I
What is betid to Cloten, but remain

15 **purposes**: intends to. **Beseech** 前省略 I.
16 **Hold me**: consider me as.
19 **subjection**: duty as a subject.
20 **wants**: is wanting, is lacking.
21 **will** 前省略 he.
22 **slip**: release, let go. **jealousy**: suspicion.
23 **depend**: impend, hang (over you).
25 **Are landed**: have landed.
27 **Now for**: if only I now had.
28 **amazed**: confused. **matter**: business.
29 **preparation**: readied forces. **affront**: confront, cope with.
30 **come more**: if more (Romans) come.
31 **want**: thing needed. **but**: only.
34 **annoy**: harm.
35 **chances**: events.
39 **yield**: give.
40 **is betid**: has happened.

Perplex'd in all. The heavens still must work.
Wherein I am false I am honest; not true, to be true.
These present wars shall find I love my country,
Even to the note o' the king, or I 'll fall in them.
All other doubts, by time let them be clear'd:
Fortune brings in some boats that are not steer'd.
[*Exit.*

SCENE IV

Wales. Before the cave of Belarius.

Enter Belarius, Guiderius, and Arviragus.

Gui. The noise is round about us.
Bel. Let us from it.
Arv. What pleasure, sir, find we in life, to lock it
From action and adventure?
Gui. Nay, what hope
Have we in hiding us? This way, the Romans
Must or for Britons slay us or receive us
For barbarous and unnatural revolts
During their use, and slay us after.
Bel. Sons,
We 'll higher to the mountains; there secure us.
To the king's party there 's no going: newness
Of Cloten's death—we being not known, not muster'd
Among the bands—may drive us to a render
Where we have lived, and so extort from 's that
Which we have done, whose answer would be death
Drawn on with torture.
Gui. This is, sir, a doubt
In such a time nothing becoming you,
Nor satisfying us.
Arv. It is not likely

44 **note**：notice.

IV. iv.

1 **from** 前省略 go.

2 **lock it**：shut it off.

4 **This way**：by this course of action.

5 **or … or**：either … or. **for**：as. 下行同。

6 **revolts**：rebels.

7 **During their use**：while we are useful to them.

8 **higher** 前省略 go. **secure**：make safe，guard from danger.

11 **bands**：troops. **render**（n.）：account.

13 **answer**：atonement，punishment.

14 **Drawn on**：prolonged.

15 **In**：at.

That when they hear the Roman horses neigh,
Behold their quarter'd fires, have both their eyes
And ears so cloy'd importantly as now,
That they will waste their time upon our note,
To know from whence we are.

Bel. O, I am known
Of many in the army: many years,
Though Cloten then but young, you see, not wore him
From my remembrance. And besides, the king
Hath not deserved my service nor your loves;
Who find in my exile the want of breeding,
The certainty of this hard life; aye hopeless
To have the courtesy your cradle promised,
But to be still hot summer's tanlings and
The shrinking slaves of winter.

Gui. Than be so
Better to cease to be. Pray, sir, to the army:
I and my brother are not known; yourself
So out of thought, and thereto so o'ergrown,
Cannot be question'd.

Arv. By this sun that shines,
I 'll thither: what thing is it that I never
Did see man die! scarce ever look'd on blood,
But that of coward hares, hot goats, and venison!
Never bestrid a horse, save one that had
A rider like myself, who ne'er wore rowel
Nor iron on his heel! I am ashamed
To look upon the holy sun, to have
The benefit of his blest beams, remaining
So long a poor unknown.

Gui. By heavens, I 'll go:
If you will bless me, sir, and give me leave,
I 'll take the better care, but if you will not,
The hazard therefore due fall on me by

18 quarter'd fires: campfires.

19 cloy'd importantly: fully occupied with important matters.

20 upon our note: in noticing us.

22 of: by.

23 then 前省略 was. **not wore**: did not wear (efface).

26 Who 指代 you. **find in my exile**: experience as a result of my exile. **want of breeding**: lack of a proper education.

27 certainty: inevitable result.

28 courtesy: cultivated existence. **cradle**: birth.

29 still: always. **tanlings**: people tanned by the sun.

30 shrinking: shivering with cold.

30—31 Than … to be: It is better to die than to be so.

33 out of thought: without being thought of. **thereto**: in addition. **o'ergrown**: covered with growth (of hair and beard).

34 question'd: inquired into.

35 I'll 后省略 go. **what thing is it**: what a disgraceful thing it is.

36 scarce: scarcely.

37 coward: timid. **hot**: lustful. **venison**: edible beasts of chase.

38 bestrid: bestride 的过去分词，骑。 **save**: except.

39 rowel: 踢马刺上的齿轮，只有绅士和骑士才在靴后跟上带踢马刺。

44 leave: permission.

46 The hazard therefore due: may the danger due to me because of my disobedience.

The hands of Romans!
Arv. So say I: amen.
Bel. No reason I, since of your lives you set
So slight a valuation, should reserve
My crack'd one to more care. Have with you, boys!
If in your country wars you chance to die,
That is my bed too, lads, and there I 'll lie:
Lead, lead. [*Aside*] The time seems long: their blood thinks scorn,
Till it fly out and show them princes born. [*Exeunt.*

48 **No reason**: there is no reason why. **of**: on, about.

50 **crack'd one**: weakened or impaired life. **Have with you**: take me with you, I'll go with you.

51 **country**, i. e., country's.

53 **thinks scorn**: disdains everything.

ACT V

SCENE I

Britain. The Roman camp.

Enter Posthumus, with a bloody handkerchief.

Post. Yea, bloody cloth, I 'll keep thee; for I wish'd
Thou shouldst be colour'd thus. You married ones,
If each of you should take this course, how many
Must murder wives much better than themselves
For wrying but a little! O Pisanio!
Every good servant does not all commands:
No bond but to do just ones. Gods! if you
Should have ta'en vengeance on my faults, I never
Had lived to put on this: so had you saved
The noble Imogen to repent, and struck
Me, wretch more worth your vengeance. But, alack,
You snatch some hence for little faults; that 's love,
To have them fall no more: you some permit
To second ills with ills, each elder worse,
And make them dread it, to the doer's thrift.
But Imogen is your own: do your best wills,
And make me blest to obey! I am brought hither
Among the Italian gentry, and to fight
Against my lady's kingdom: 'tis enough
That, Britain, I have kill'd thy mistress; peace!
I 'll give no wound to thee. Therefore, good heavens,
Hear patiently my purpose: I 'll disrobe me
Of these Italian weeds, and suit myself
As does a Briton peasant: so I 'll fight

V. i.

5 **wrying**：deviating from virtue，erring.

6 **does not**：does not perform.

7 **bond**：obligation. **but**：except.

9 **put on**：instigate.

12 **some**：some people.

13 **fall**：sin.

14 **second**：follow up. **elder**：later fault (ill).

15 **thrift**：advantage，benefit.

16 **your** 指 God's. 从 7 行后半开始，一直是对 God 说话。

20 **peace**：silence.

23 **weeds**：clothes. **suit** (v. t.)：clothe.

Against the part I come with; so I 'll die
For thee, O Imogen, even for whom my life
Is, every breath, a death: and thus, unknown,
Pitied nor hated, to the face of peril
Myself I 'll dedicate. Let me make men know
More valour in me than my habits show.
Gods, put the strength o' the Leonati in me!
To shame the guise o' the world, I will begin
The fashion, less without and more within. [*Exit.*

SCENE II

Field of battle between the British and Roman camps.

Enter, from one side, Lucius, Iachimo, Imogen, and the Roman army; from the other side, the British army; Leonatus Posthumus following, like a poor soldier. They march over and go out. Then enter again, in skirmish, Iachimo and Posthumus: he vanquisheth and disarmeth Iachimo, and then leaves him.

Iach. The heaviness and guilt within my bosom
Takes off my manhood: I have belied a lady,
The princess of this country, and the air on 't
Revengingly enfeebles me; or could this carl,
A very drudge of nature's, have subdued me
In my profession? Knighthoods and honours, borne
As I wear mine, are titles but of scorn.
If that thy gentry, Britain, go before
This lout as he exceeds our lords, the odds
Is that we scarce are men and you are gods. [*Exit.*

The battle continues; the Britons fly; Cymbeline is taken; then enter, to his rescue, Belarius, Guiderius, and Arviragus.

Bel. Stand, stand! We have the advantage of the ground;

25 **part**：party，side.

28 **Pitied**，i. e.，neither pitied.

30 **habits**：garments.

31 **Leonati**：Leonatus 家族(拉丁复数)。

32 **guise**：custom.

V. ii.

1 **heaviness and guilt**，两个抽象名词视为单数。

2 **belied**：slandered.

3 **on 't**：of it.

4 **or**：otherwise. **carl**：churl，peasant.

5 **very**：mere. **drudge**：slave.

7 **but**：merely. **of scorn**：contemptible.

8 **go before**：surpass.

9 **lout**：bumpkin.

10 **scarce**：scarcely.

The lane is guarded: nothing routs us but
The villany of our fears.

Gui.
Arv. } Stand, stand, and fight!

Re-enter Posthumus, and seconds the Britons: they rescue Cymbeline and exeunt. Then re-enter Lucius, Iachimo, and Imogen.

Luc. Away, boy, from the troops, and save thyself;
For friends kill friends, and the disorder 's such
As war were hoodwink'd.

Iach. 'Tis their fresh supplies.

Luc. It is a day turn'd strangely: or betimes
Let 's reinforce, or fly. [*Exeunt.*

SCENE III

Another part of the field.

Enter Posthumus and a British Lord.

Lord. Camest thou from where they made the stand?

Post. I did:
Though you, it seems, come from the fliers.

Lord. I did.

Post. No blame be to you, sir; for all was lost,
But that the heavens fought: the king himself
Of his wings destitute, the army broken,
And but the backs of Britons seen, all flying
Through a strait lane; the enemy full-hearted,
Lolling the tongue with slaughtering, having work
More plentiful than tools to do 't, struck down
Some mortally, some slightly touch'd, some falling
Merely through fear; that the strait pass was damm'd
With dead men hurt behind, and cowards living

16 As: as if. **hoodwink'd**: blindfolded.

17 or betimes: either promptly.

V. iii.

4 But: had it not been.

5 Of his wings destitute: deprived of the supporting forces on either side of him.

6 but: only.

7 strait: narrow. **full-hearted**: with high courage and confidence.

8 Lolling: hanging out.

10 touch'd: wounded.

12 behind: from behind, on their backs.

To die with lengthen'd shame.
Lord. Where was this lane?
Post. Close by the battle, ditch'd, and wall'd with turf;
Which gave advantage to an ancient soldier,
An honest one, I warrant; who deserved
So long a breeding as his white beard came to,
In doing this for 's country. Athwart the lane
He, with two striplings—lads more like to run
The country base than to commit such slaughter;
With faces fit for masks, or rather fairer
Than those for preservation cased, or shame—
Made good the passage; cried to those that fled,
'Our Britain's harts die flying, not our men:
To darkness fleet souls that fly backwards. Stand;
Or we are Romans, and will give you that
Like beasts which you shun beastly, and may save
But to look back in frown: stand, stand!'These three,
Three thousand confident, in act as many,—
For three performers are the file when all
The rest do nothing,—with this word 'Stand, stand,'
Accommodated by the place, more charming
With their own nobleness, which could have turn'd
A distaff to a lance, gilded pale looks,
Part shame, part spirit renew'd; that some, turn'd coward
But by example,—O, a sin in war,
Damn'd in the first beginners! —'gan to look
The way that they did, and to grin like lions
Upon the pikes o' the hunters. Then began
A stop i' the chaser, a retire; anon
A rout, confusion thick: forthwith they fly
Chickens, the way which they stoop'd eagles; slaves,
The strides they victors made: and now our cowards,
Like fragments in hard voyages, became

13 **die with lengthen'd shame**: die later after a life of prolonged shame.

16 **honest**: worthy.

17 to be supported for as long again as his white beard indicated he had already lived.

18 **Athwart**: across.

19 **like**: likely.

20 **country base**: a rural children's game (prisoner's base) that involves running between two bases.

21 **fit for masks**: worthy to be protected against sun and wind.

22 **those … shame**: ladies' faces masked to preserve complexion or for modesty.

23 **Made good**: secured.

24 **harts**: deer.

25 **darkness**: hell. **fleet** (v. i.): rush. **fly**: flee.

26 **Or we are Romans**: otherwise we will behave like Romans. **that**, i. e., death.

27 **shun beastly**: try to escape from in a beastly manner. **save**: spare your life.

28 **But**: only. **to look**: by looking. **in frown**: with threatening face.

29 **Three thousand confident**: as confident as if they were three thousand.

30 **file**: entire force.

32 **Accommodated**: favoured. **charming**: acting like a charm (magic) on others.

34 **distaff**: 纺锤，象征妇女。 **gilded**: brought colour to.

35 **Part … renew'd**: shame revived some, courage others.

37 **first beginners**: those who first started to run away. **'gan**: began.

38 **they**, i. e., the three. **grin**: bare their teeth.

40 **retire**: retreat. **anon**: soon.

41 **forthwith**: straightaway. **fly**: flee.

42 **Chickens**: like chickens. **the way which**: along the passage down which. **stoop'd**: swooped. **eagles**: like eagles. **slaves**: like slaves.

43 **The strides**: along the steps (主语仍为 they fly). **they victors made**: which they made as victors.

44 **fragments**: bits of food.

The life o' the need: having found the back-door open
Of the unguarded hearts, heavens, how they wound!
Some slain before, some dying, some their friends
O'er-borne i' the former wave: ten chased by one
Are now each one the slaughter-man of twenty:
Those that would die or ere resist are grown
The mortal bugs o' the field.

Lord. This was strange chance:
A narrow lane, an old man, and two boys.

Post. Nay, do not wonder at it: you are made
Rather to wonder at the things you hear
Than to work any. Will you rhyme upon 't,
And vent it for a mockery? Here is one:
'Two boys, an old man twice a boy, a lane,
Preserved the Britons, was the Romans' bane.

Lord. Nay, be not angry, sir.

Post. 'Lack, to what end?
Who dares not stand his foe, I 'll be his friend;
For if he 'll do as he is made to do,
I know he 'll quickly fly my friendship too.
You have put me into rhyme.

Lord. Farewell; you 're angry. [*Exit.*

Post. Still going? This is a lord! O noble misery!
To be i' the field, and ask 'what news?' of me!
To-day how many would have given their honours
To have saved their carcasses! Took heel to do 't,
And yet died too! I, in mine own woe charm'd,
Could not find death where I did hear him groan,
Nor feel him where he struck. Being an ugly monster,
'Tis strange he hides him in fresh cups, soft beds,
Sweet words; or hath moe ministers than we
That draw his knives i' the war. Well, I will find him:
For being now a favourer to the Briton,
No more a Briton, I have resumed again

45 **life o' the need**: source of existence in distress.

45—46 **back-door … hearts**: weak spot of the undefended souls (Romans) unprotected.

46 **wound** (v. i.): inflict wounds.

48 **O'er-borne**: overwhelmed.

50 **or ere**: before they would.

51 **bugs**: bugbears, terrors. **chance**: good fortune.

55 **work**: perform. **rhyme**: compose verses.

56 **vent**: circulate. **it**, i. e., your poetry, verses. **mockery**: subject of laughter.

57 **twice a boy**: in his second childhood.

60 **stand**: withstand, confront.

61 **made**: inclined.

62 **fly**: leave, desert.

63 **put**: forced.

64 **Still going**: always running away. **misery**: wretchedness.

68 **too**: anyway. **charm'd**: preserved, as if by a charm.

69 **him**, i. e., death,下面几行同。

72 **moe**: more, other. **ministers**: agents.

74 **For … Briton**: since death now favours the Britons.

75 **No … I**: I, no longer a Briton.

The part I came in: fight I will no more,
But yield me to the veriest hind that shall
Once touch my shoulder. Great the slaughter is
Here made by the Roman; great the answer be
Britons must take. For me, my ransom 's death:
On either side I come to spend my breath,
Which neither here I 'll keep nor bear again,
But end it by some means for Imogen.

Enter two British Captains and Soldiers.

First Cap. Great Jupiter be praised! Lucius is taken:
'Tis thought the old man and his sons were angels.
Sec. Cap. There was a fourth man, in a silly habit,
That gave the affront with them.
First Cap. So 'tis reported:
But none of 'em can be found. Stand! who 's there?
Post. A Roman;
Who had not now been drooping here if seconds
Had answer'd him.
Sec. Cap. Lay hands on him; a dog!
A leg of Rome shall not return to tell
What crows have peck'd them here. He brags his service
As if he were of note: bring him to the king.

Enter Cymbeline, Belarius, Guiderius, Arviragus, Pisanio, and Roman Captives. The Captains present Posthumus to Cymbeline, who delivers him over to a Gaoler: then exeunt omnes.

SCENE IV

A British prison.

Enter Posthumus and two Gaolers.

First Gaol. You shall not now be stol'n, you have

76 **part**: role.

77 **veriest**: very first. **hind**: peasant.

78 **touch my shoulder**: try to arrest me.

79 **great the answer be**: may great be the retaliation that.

80 **For me**: as for me.

81 **spend my breath**: give up my life.

82 **neither here I'll keep**: I'll neither keep here. **bear**: carry away.

86 **silly habit**: rustic garment.

87 **gave the affront**: faced the enemy.

90 **had not … drooping**: would not have been languishing. **seconds**: supporters.

91 **answer'd him**: followed his example.

92 **leg**: lag, lowest class.

94 **note**: high rank.

S. D. **exeunt omnes** [拉丁]: all go out.

V. iv.

1 **locks**: fetters, shackles.

locks upon you:
So graze as you find pasture.
Sec. Gaol. Ay, or a stomach.
[*Exeunt Gaolers.*

Post. Most welcome, bondage! for thou art a way,
I think, to liberty: yet am I better
Than one that 's sick o' the gout; since he had rather
Groan so in perpetuity than be cured
By the sure physician, death, who is the key
To unbar these locks. My conscience, thou art fetter'd
More than my shanks and wrists: you good gods, give me
The penitent instrument to pick that bolt,
Then, free for ever! Is 't enough I am sorry?
So children temporal fathers do appease;
Gods are more full of mercy. Must I repent?
I cannot do it better than in gyves,
Desired more than constrain'd: to satisfy,
If of my freedom 'tis the main part, take
No stricter render of me than my all.
I know you are more clement than vile men,
Who of their broken debtors take a third,
A sixth, a tenth, letting them thrive again
On their abatement: that 's not my desire:
For Imogen's dear life take mine; and though
'Tis not so dear, yet 'tis a life; you coin'd it:
'Tween man and man they weigh not every stamp;
Though light, take pieces for the figure's sake:
You rather mine, being yours: and so, great powers,
If you will take this audit, take this life,
And cancel these cold bonds. O Imogen!
I 'll speak to thee in silence. [*Sleeps.*

2 **stomach**：appetite.

5 **gout**：痛风病。

8 **unbar**：unfasten.

10 **penitent … bolt**：key of penitence to unlock the door-bar on my conscience.

12 **temporal**：of this world.

15 **constrain'd**：forced on me. **satisfy**：atone.

16 **of my freedom … part**：the principal element in freeing me from guilt.

17 **render**：repayment. **of**：from.

18 **clement**：kind，merciful.

19 **broken**：bankrupt.

21 **abatement**：reduced principal.

23 **so dear**：as valuable as hers. **coin'd**：created.

24 **stamp**：coin.

25 **light**：deficient in weight. **take … sake**：they accept the coins because of the image (of the King) stamped on them.

26 **rather**，i. e.，should rather take (my life). **being yours**：being made in God's image.

27 **audit**：final account.

28 **cold bonds**：(1) insensible contract by which the term of life is held；(2) harsh prison fetters，双关。

Solemn music. Enter, as in an apparition, Sicilius Leonatus, father to Posthumus, an old man, attired like a warrior; leading in his hand an ancient matron, his wife and mother to Posthumus, with music before them: then, after other music, follow the two young Leonati, brothers to Posthumus, with wounds as they died in the wars. They circle Posthumus round as he lies sleeping.

Sici. No more, thou thunder-master, show
Thy spite on mortal flies:
With Mars fall out, with Juno chide,
That thy adulteries
Rates and revenges.
Hath my poor boy done aught but well,
Whose face I never saw?
I died whilst in the womb he stay'd
Attending nature's law:
Whose father then—as men report
Thou orphans' father art—
Thou shouldst have been, and shielded him
From this earth-vexing smart.

Moth. Lucina lent not me her aid,
But took me in my throes;
That from me was Posthumus ript,
Came crying 'mongst his foes,
A thing of pity!

Sici. Great nature, like his ancestry,
Moulded the stuff so fair,
That he deserved the praise o' the world,
As great Sicilius' heir.

First Bro. When once he was mature for man,
In Britain where was he

30 thunder-master：罗马神话中的天帝 Jove，司雷电。

31 mortal flies，神蔑视凡人如同苍蝇。

32 Mars：罗马神话中的战神。 **Juno**：罗马神话中的天后。 **chide**：quarrel.

33 That：who，i. e.，Juno. **adulteries**：Jove 有许多婚外韵事。

34 Rates：berates，scolds.

35 boy，i. e.，Posthumus.

38 law：decree.

40 Thou orphans' father art，此处 thou 本指 Jove，但又和基督教的上帝相混，见《旧约圣经·诗篇》68：5，"上帝在他的圣所作孤儿的父"。

42 earth-vexing smart：suffering that afflicts mortals.

43 Lucina：罗马神话中的生育女神。

44 took me：took my life.

49 stuff：substance.

52 for man：as a grown-up.

53 he：the man.

That could stand up his parallel,
Or fruitful object be
In eye of Imogen, that best
Could deem his dignity?

Moth. With marriage wherefore was he mock'd
To be exiled, and thrown
From Leonati seat, and cast
From her his dearest one,
Sweet Imogen?

Sici. Why did you suffer Iachimo,
Slight thing of Italy,
To taint his nobler heart and brain
With needless jealousy;
And to become the geck and scorn
O' the other's villany?

Sec. Bro. For this, from stiller seats we came,
Our parents and us twain,
That striking in our country's cause
Fell bravely and were slain,
Our fealty and Tenantius' right
With honour to maintain.

First Bro. Like hardiment Posthumus hath
To Cymbeline perform'd:
Then, Jupiter, thou king of gods,
Why hast thou thus adjourn'd
The graces for his merits due;
Being all to dolours turn'd?

Sici. Thy crystal window ope; look out;
No longer exercise
Upon a valiant race thy harsh
And potent injuries.

Moth. Since, Jupiter, our son is good,

55 **fruitful**：life-giving.

57 **deem**：judge. **dignity**：worth.

58 **wherefore**：why.

60 **Leonati seat**：the estate of Leonatus.

63 **you**，i. e.，the Gods.

64 **Slight**：worthless.

67 **geck**：dupe.

69 **stiller seats**：calmer regions，i. e.，Elysium，abode of the blessed after death，见下 97 行。

71 **striking**：fighting.

73 **fealty**：loyalty. **Tenantius**：Cymbeline's father.

75 **Like hardiment**：similar deeds of valour.

76 **To**：for.

77 **Jupiter**：Jove 别名。

78 **adjourn'd**：deferred，delayed.

79 **graces**：favours.

80 **dolours**：sorrows.

81 **ope**：open.

82 **exercise**：perform，practise.

Take off his miseries.

Sici. Peep through thy marble mansion; help;
Or we poor ghosts will cry
To the shining synod of the rest
Against thy deity.

Both Bro. Help, Jupiter; or we appeal,
And from thy justice fly.

Jupiter descends in thunder and lightning, sitting upon an eagle: he throws a thunderbolt. The Ghosts fall on their knees.

Jup. No more, you petty spirits of region low,
Offend our hearing; hush! How dare you ghosts
Accuse the thunderer, whose bolt, you know,
Sky-planted, batters all rebelling coasts?
Poor shadows of Elysium, hence, and rest
Upon your never-withering banks of flowers:
Be not with mortal accidents opprest;
No care of yours it is; you know 'tis ours.
Whom best I love I cross; to make my gift,
The more delay'd, delighted. Be content;
Your low-laid son our godhead will uplift:
His comforts thrive, his trials well are spent.
Our Jovial star reign'd at his birth, and in
Our temple was he married. Rise, and fade.
He shall be lord of lady Imogen,
And happier much by his affliction made.
This tablet lay upon his breast, wherein
Our pleasure his full fortune doth confine:
And so away: no farther with your din
Express impatience, lest you stir up mine.
Mount, eagle, to my palace crystalline. [*Ascends.*

Sici. He came in thunder; his celestial breath

89 **synod**: assembly. **the rest**, i. e., the other gods.

96 **Sky-planted**: rooted in the heavens.

97 **Elysium**,见上 69 行注。

99 **accidents**: events.

101 **cross**: thwart.

102 **delighted**, i. e., the more delighted in.

104 **spent**: ended.

105 **Jovial star**: the planet Jupiter,木星。

110 It is our pleasure that it specifies his great fortune.

112 **mine**, i. e., my impatience.

Was sulphurous to smell: the holy eagle
Stoop'd, as to foot us: his ascension is
More sweet than our blest fields: his royal bird
Prunes the immortal wing and cloys his beak,
As when his god is pleased.

All. Thanks, Jupiter!

Sici. The marble pavement closes, he is enter'd
His radiant roof. Away! And, to be blest,
Let us with care perform his great behest.
[*The Ghosts vanish.*

Post. [*Waking*] Sleep, thou hast been a grandsire, and begot
A father to me; and thou hast created
A mother and two brothers: but, O scorn!
Gone! They went hence so soon as they were born:
And so I am awake. Poor wretches that depend
On greatness' favour dream as I have done;
Wake, and find nothing. But, alas, I swerve:
Many dream not to find, neither deserve,
And yet are steep'd in favours; so am I,
That have this golden chance, and know not why.
What fairies haunt this ground? A book? O rare one!
Be not, as is our fangled world, a garment
Nobler than that it covers: let thy effects
So follow, to be most unlike our courtiers,
As good as promise.

[*Reads*] 'When as a lion's whelp shall, to himself unknown, without seeking find, and be embraced by a piece. of tender air, and when from a stately cedar shall be lopped branches, which, being dead many years, shall after revive, be jointed to the old stock and freshly grow, then shall Posthumus end his miseries, Britain be

116 Stoop'd, as to foot us: swooped as if to seize us in its claws.

118 Prunes: preens, arranges plumage with the bill. **cloys**: strokes with a claw.

120 pavement: floor of the heavens (a trapdoor in the ceiling of the stage). **is enter'd**: has entered.

125 scorn: mockery.

128 greatness' favour dream: dream of favour from powerful men.

129 swerve: go astray, err.

130 dream not to find: do not dream of finding favour.

133 book,即前面 109 行所说的 tablet. **rare**: exceptionally fine.

134 fangled: foppish, given to finery and fashions.

135 that: what.

136 to be: that they.

138 When as: when.

140 piece: portion, puff.

141 cedar: 雪松。

142 after: afterwards.

143 jointed: joined.

fortunate and flourish in peace and plenty.'

'Tis still a dream; or else such stuff as madmen
Tongue, and brain not: either both, or nothing:
Or senseless speaking, or a speaking such
As sense cannot untie. Be what it is,
The action of my life is like it, which
I'll keep, if but for sympathy.

Re-enter Gaolers.

First Gaol. Come, sir, are you ready for death?

Post. Over-roasted rather; ready long ago.

First Gaol. Hanging is the word, sir: if you be ready for that, you are well cooked.

Post. So, if I prove a good repast to the spectators, the dish pays the shot.

First Gaol. A heavy reckoning for you, sir. But the comfort is, you shall be called to no more payments, fear no more tavern-bills; which are often the sadness of parting, as the procuring of mirth: you come in faint for want of meat, depart reeling with too much drink; sorry that you have paid too much, and sorry that you are paid too much; purse and brain both empty, the brain the heavier for being too light, the purse too light, being drawn of heaviness: of this contradiction you shall now be quit. O, the charity of a penny cord! it sums up thousands in a trice: you have no true debitor and creditor but it; of what 's past, is, and to come, the discharge: your neck, sir, is pen, book and counters; so the acquittance follows.

Post. I am merrier to die than thou art to live.

First Gaol. Indeed, sir, he that sleeps feels not the toothache: but a man that were to sleep your

147 **Tongue**: speak. **brain**: understand.

148 **speaking**: speech.

149 **sense**: reason. **untie**: solve, interpret. **Be what it is**: be it what it is.

150 **action**: strenuous activity.

151 **but**: only. **for sympathy**: because of the similarity.

153 **over-roasted**: overripe.

157 **shot**: reckoning, bill.

165 **paid**: punished, subdued (by drink).

166 **heavier**: sleepier. **light**: foolish.

167 **drawn**: emptied.

170 **debitor and creditor**: accountant, account book.

171 **discharge**: release from debt.

172 **counters**: metal tokens used for making calculations.

173 **acquittance**: acquittal, clearance.

sleep, and a hangman to help him to bed, I think he would change places with his officer; for, look you, sir, you know not which way you shall go.

Post. Yes, indeed do I, fellow.

First Gaol. Your death has eyes in 's head then; I have not seen him so pictured: you must either be directed by some that take upon them to know, or to take upon yourself that which I am sure you do not know, or jump the after-inquiry on your own peril: and how you shall speed in your journey's end, I think you 'll never return to tell one.

Post. I tell thee, fellow, there are none want eyes to direct them the way I am going, but such as wink and will not use them.

First Gaol. What an infinite mock is this, that a man should have the best use of eyes to see the way of blindness! I am sure hanging 's the way of winking.

Enter a Messenger.

Mess. Knock off his manacles; bring your prisoner to the king.

Post. Thou bringest good news, I am called to be made free.

First Gaol. I 'll be hanged then.

Post. Thou shalt be then freer than a gaoler ; no bolts for the dead. [*Exeunt all but First Gaoler.*

First Gaol. Unless a man would marry a gallows and beget young gibbets, I never saw one so prone. Yet, on my conscience, there are verier knaves desire to live, for all he be a Roman: and there be some of them too, that die against their wills;

177 **a hangman to help**: that a hangman being ready to help.

178 **he**,此字多余。 **officer**: executioner.

182 **death**,死之图形,其骷髅眼孔中一般无眼珠。

184 **take upon them**: profess.

185 **take upon yourself**: pretend to know.

186 **jump**: risk.

187 **speed**: succeed.

189 **one**: on, of.

190 **want**: who lack.

192 **wink**: shut their eyes.

195 **of blindness**: to death.

200 **made free**, i. e., set free by death.

205 **prone**: eagerly ready (to die).

206 **verier**: more truly. **knaves** 后省略 who.

207 **for all**: even though, despite that. **Roman**:一般认为罗马人持斯多葛派 Stoics 态度,对死亡不在乎。

so should I, if I were one. I would we were all of one mind, and one mind good; O, there were desolation of gaolers and gallowses! I speak against my present profit, but my wish hath a preferment in 't. [*Exit.*

SCENE V

Cymbeline's tent.

Enter Cymbeline, Belarius, Guiderius, Arviragus, Pisanio, Lords, Officers, and Attendants.

Cym. Stand by my side, you whom the gods have made
Preservers of my throne. Woe is my heart,
That the poor soldier, that so richly fought,
Whose rags shamed gilded arms, whose naked breast
Stepp'd before targes of proof, cannot be found:
He shall be happy that can find him, if
Our grace can make him so.

Bel. I never saw
Such noble fury in so poor a thing;
Such precious deeds in one that promised nought
But beggary and poor looks.

Cym. No tidings of him?

Pis. He hath been search'd among the dead and living,
But no trace of him.

Cym. To my grief, I am
The heir of his reward; [*To Belarius, Guiderius, and Arviragus*] which I will add
To you, the liver, heart, and brain of Britain,
By whom I grant she lives. 'Tis now the time
To ask of whence you are: report it.

Bel. Sir,
In Cambria are we born, and gentlemen

209 **one**, i. e., a Roman. **would**: wish.

211 **desolation**: destitution, ruin.

213 **preferment**: promotion, better fortune.

V. v.

2 **Woe is my heart**: woe is to my heart.

3 **richly**: splendidly.

5 **targes of proof**: shields of tested strength.

7 **Our grace**: my favour.

15 **grant**: admit.

Further to boast were neither true nor modest,
Unless I add we are honest.

Cym. Bow you knees.
Arise my knights o' the battle: I create you
Companions to our person, and will fit you
With dignities becoming your estates.

Enter Cornelius and Ladies.

There 's business in these faces. Why so sadly
Greet you our victory? you look like Romans,
And not o' the court of Britain.

Cor. Hail, great king!
To sour your happiness, I must report
The queen is dead.

Cym. Who worse than a physician
Would this report become? But I consider,
By medicine life may be prolong'd, yet death
Will seize the doctor too. How ended she?

Cor. With horror, madly dying, like her life;
Which, being cruel to the world, concluded
Most cruel to herself. What she confess'd
I will report, so please you: these her women
Can trip me if I err; who with wet cheeks
Were present when she finish'd.

Cym. Prithee, say.

Cor. First, she confess'd she never loved you, only
Affected greatness got by you, not you:
Married your royalty, was wife to your place,
Abhorr'd your person.

Cym. She alone knew this;
And, but she spoke in dying, I would not
Believe her lips in opening it. Proceed.

Cor. Your daughter, whom she bore in hand to love
With such integrity, she did confess

21 **fit**: furnish.

22 **estates**: rank.

28 **become**: befit.

34 **so please you**: if it pleases you to do so.

35 **trip**: refute.

38 **Affected**: desired, loved.

39 **place**: position.

41 **but**: except that, unless.

42 **opening**: revealing.

43 **bore in hand**: pretended.

44 **integrity**: honesty.

Was as a scorpion to her sight; whose life,
But that her flight prevented it, she had
Ta'en off by poison.

Cym. O most delicate fiend!
Who is 't can read a woman? Is there more?

Cor. More, sir, and worse. She did confess she had
For you a mortal mineral; which, being took,
Should by the minute feed on life and lingering
By inches waste you: in which time she purposed,
By watching, weeping, tendance, kissing, to
O'ercome you with her show, and in time,
When she had fitted you with her craft, to work
Her son into the adoption of the crown:
But, failing of her end by his strange absence,
Grew shameless-desperate; open'd, in despite
Of heaven and men, her purposes; repented
The evils she hatch'd were not effected; so
Despairing died.

Cym. Heard you all this, her women?

Ladies. We did, so please your highness.

Cym. Mine eyes
Were not in fault, for she was beautiful,
Mine ears that heard her flattery, nor my heart
That thought her like her seeming; it had been vicious
To have mistrusted her: yet, O my daughter
That it was folly in me, thou mayst say,
And prove it in thy feeling. Heaven mend all!

Enter Lucius, Iachimo, the Soothsayer, and other Roman Prisoners, guarded; Posthumus behind, and Imogen.

Thou comest not, Caius, now for tribute; that
The Britons have razed out, though with the loss
Of many a bold one; whose kinsmen have made suit
That their good souls may be appeased with slaughter

47 **delicate**: subtle.

50 **mineral**: substance, poison. **took**: taken.

53 **watching**: staying awake. **tendance**: attendance, attention.

55 **fitted you with**: shaped you by.

58 **open'd**: revealed.

65 **seeming**: appearance. **vicious**: wrong.

68 **in thy feeling**: by your experience.

70 **razed out**: erased (that=the tribute).

Of you their captives, which ourself have granted:
So think of your estate.

Luc. Consider, sir, the chance of war: the day
Was yours by accident; had it gone with us,
We should not, when the blood was cool, have threaten'd
Our prisoners with the sword. But since the gods
Will have it thus, that nothing but our lives
May be call'd ransom, let it come: sufficeth
A Roman with a Roman's heart can suffer:
Augustus lives to think on 't: and so much
For my peculiar care. This one thing only
I will entreat; my boy, a Briton born,
Let him be ransom'd: never master had
A page so kind, so duteous, diligent,
So tender over his occasions, true,
So feat, so nurse-like: let his virtue join
With my request, which I 'll make bold your highness
Cannot deny; he hath done no Briton harm,
Though he have served a Roman: save him, sir,
And spare no blood beside.

Cym. I have surely seen him:
His favour is familiar to me. Boy,
Thou hast look'd thyself into my grace,
And art mine own. I know not why, nor wherefore,
To say, live, boy: ne'er thank thy master; live:
And ask of Cymbeline what boon thou wilt,
Fitting my bounty and thy state, I 'll give it;
Yea, though thou do demand a prisoner,
The noblest ta'en.

Imo. I humbly thank your highness.

Luc. I do not bid thee beg my life, good lad,
And yet I know thou wilt.

Imo. No, no: alack,
There 's other work in hand: I see a thing

74 **estate**: condition, situation.

82 **think on 't**: consider what to do.

83 **my peculiar care**: concern for myself.

85 **never master**: never a master.

87 **tender over his occasions**: thoughtful of his needs.

88 **feat** (adj.): dexterous, neat.

92 **And**: even if you. **no blood beside**: no one else.

93 **favour**: face.

94 **look'd thyself into my grace**: by your appearance gained my favour.

97 **boon**: favour begged. 下 135 行同。

103 **thing**, i. e., the ring she gave Posthumus and now on Iachimo's finger.

Bitter to me as death: your life, good master,
Must shuffle for itself.

Luc. The boy disdains me,
He leaves me, scorns me: briefly die their joys
That place them on the truth of girls and boys.
Why stands he so perplex'd?

Cym. What wouldst thou, boy?
I love thee more and more: think more and more
What's best to ask. Know'st him thou look'st on?
Speak,
Wilt have him live? Is he thy kin? thy friend?

Imo. He is a Roman; no more kin to me
Than I to your highness; who, being born your vassal,
Am something nearer.

Cym. Wherefore eyest him so?

Imo. I 'll tell you, sir, in private, if you please
To give me hearing.

Cym. Ay, with all my heart,
And lend my best attention. What 's thy name?

Imo. Fidele, sir.

Cym. Thou 'rt my good youth, my page;
I 'll be thy master: walk with me; speak freely.
[*Cymbeline and Imogen converse apart.*

Bel. Is not this boy revived from death?

Arv. One sand another
Not more resembles that sweet rosy lad
Who died, and was Fidele. What think you?

Gui. The same dead thing alive.

Bel. Peace, peace! See further; he eyes us not; forbear;
Creatures may be alike: were 't he, I am sure
He would have spoke to us.

Gui. But we saw him dead.

Bel. Be silent; let 's see further.

Pis. [*Aside*] It is my mistress:

107 **them**, i. e., their joys. **truth**: fidelity.

120 **sand**: grain of sand.

126 **spoke**: spoken.

Since she is living, let the time run on.
To good or bad.
[*Cymbeline and Imogen come forward.*
Cym. Come, stand thou by our side;
Make thy demand aloud. [*To Iachimo*] Sir, step you forth;
Give answer to this boy, and do it freely;
Or, by our greatness and the grace of it,
Which is our honour, bitter torture shall
Winnow the truth from falsehood. On, speak to him.
Imo. My boon is that this gentleman may render
Of whom he had this ring.
Post. [*Aside*] What 's that to him?
Cym. That diamond upon your finger, say
How came it yours?
Iach. Thou 'lt torture me to leave unspoken that
Which, to be spoke, would torture thee.
Cym. How! me?
Iach. I am glad to be constrain'd to utter that
Which torments me to conceal. By villany
I got this ring: 'twas Leonatus' jewel;
Whom thou didst banish; and—which more may grieve thee,
As it doth me,—a nobler sir ne'er lived
'Twixt sky and ground. Wilt thou hear more, my lord?
Cym. All that belongs to this.
Iach. That paragon, thy daughter,
For whom my heart drops blood and my false spirits
Quail to remember—Give me leave; I faint.
Cym. My daughter? what of her? Renew thy strength:
I had rather thou shouldst live while nature will
Than die ere I hear more: strive, man, and speak.
Iach. Upon a time—unhappy was the clock
That struck the hour! —it was in Rome,—accurst

131 **freely**: honestly.

132 **Or**: otherwise.

134 **Winnow**: separate.

135 **render**: declare.

136 **Of**: from.

138 **yours** 前省略 to be.

139 **Thou 'lt**: you will, you wish to. **to leave**: for leaving.

140 **to be spoke**: by being spoken.

145 **sir**: man.

151 **will**: allows.

The mansion where! —'twas at a feast,—O, would
Our viands had been poison'd, or at least
Those which I heaved to head! —the good Posthumus,—
What should I say? he was too good to be
Where ill men were; and was the best of all
Amongst the rarest of good ones—sitting sadly,
Hearing us praise our loves of Italy
For beauty that made barren the swell'd boast
Of him that best could speak; for feature, laming
The shrine of Venus, or straight-pight Minerva,
Postures beyond brief nature; for condition,
A shop of all the qualities that man
Loves woman for; besides that hook of wiving,
Fairness which strikes the eye—

Cym. I stand on fire:
Come to the matter.

Iach. All too soon I shall,
Unless thou wouldst grieve quickly. This Posthumus,
Most like a noble lord in love and one
That had a royal lover, took his hint,
And not dispraising whom we praised,—therein
He was as calm as virtue—he began
His mistress' picture; which by his tongue being made,
And then a mind put in 't, either our brags
Were crack'd of kitchen-trulls, or his description
Proved us unspeaking sots.

Cym. Nay, nay, to the purpose.

Iach. Your daughter's chastity—there it begins.
He spake of her, as Dian had hot dreams,
And she alone were cold: whereat I, wretch,
Made scruple of his praise, and wager'd with him
Pieces of gold 'gainst this which then he wore
Upon his honour'd finger, to attain

157 **heaved to head**：lifted to my mouth.

161 **our loves**：women beloved by us.

162 **barren**：dull. **swell'd**：exaggerated.

163 **feature**：form，figure. **laming**：making … look lame by comparison.

164 **shrine**：image. **straight-pight**：erect. **pight** 为 pitch 的过去分词。 **Minerva**：罗马神话中智慧和文艺的女神。

165 **brief**：short-living，mortal. **condition**：character.

166 **shop**：storehouse.

167 **hook of wiving**：bait for marriage.

169 **matter**：substance. **All too**：all 强调词。

172 **hint**：occasion.

173 **dispraising**：censuring，denigrating.

176 **put in 't**：inserted into the picture.

177 **crack'd**：boastly spoken. **kitchen-trulls**：kitchen-wenches，low women.

178 **unspeaking sots**：fools unable to describe (beauty).

180 **spake**：spoke. **as**：as if. **Dian**：Diana，贞洁女神。 **hot**：lustful.

182 **Made scruple**：expressed doubt.

183 **this**，i. e.，this ring.

In suit the place of 's bed and win this ring
By hers and mine adultery: he, true knight,
No lesser of her honour confident
Than I did truly find her, stakes this ring;
And would so, had it been a carbuncle
Of Phœbus' wheel; and might so safely, had it
Been all the worth of 's car. Away to Britain
Post I in this design: well may you, sir,
Remember me at court; where I was taught
Of your chaste daughter the wide difference
'Twixt amorous and villanous. Being thus quench'd
Of hope, not longing, mine Italian brain
'Gan in your duller Britain operate
Most vilely; for my vantage, excellent;
And, to be brief, my practice so prevail'd,
That I return'd with simular proof enough
To make the noble Leonatus mad,
By wounding his belief in her renown
With tokens thus, and thus; averring notes
Of chamber-hanging, pictures, this her bracelet,—
O cunning, how I got it! —nay, some marks
Of secret on her person, that he could not
But think her bond of chastity quite crack'd,
I having ta'en the forfeit. Whereupon—
Methinks I see him now—

Post. [*Advancing*] Ay, so thou dost,
Italian fiend! Ay me, most credulous fool,
Egregious murderer, thief, any thing
That 's due to all the villains past, in being,
To come! O, give me cord, or knife, or poison,
Some upright justicer! Thou, king, send out
For torturers ingenious: it is I
That all the abhorred things o' the earth amend
By being worse than they. I am Posthumus,

185 **In suit**：by urging my suit.

186 **By**：through. **hers and mine**：her and my.

189 **carbuncle**：ruby.

190 **Phœbus' wheel**：a wheel of the sun-god's chariot.

192 **Post**：hasten.

194 **Of**：by.

195 **quench'd**：checked.

196 **not longing**：though not of desire.

197 **'Gan**：began. **duller Britain**：Britain's northerly climate was supposed to make her people sluggish and dull-witted.

198 **vantage**：profit，gain.

199 **practice**：treacherous scheme.

200 **simular**：pretended，specious.

202 **renown**：good name.

203 **averring**：alleging，citing.

208 **forfeit**：因被罚而丧失之物，what was forfeited by the broken bond—her chastity.

211 **Egregious**：flagrant.

212 **in being**：now in existence.

214 **justicer**：judge.

216 **amend**：make (things) look better.

That kill'd thy daughter: villain-like, I lie;
That caused a lesser villain than myself,
A sacrilegious thief, to do 't. The temple
Of virtue was she; yea, and she herself.
Spit, and throw stones, cast mire upon me, set
The dogs o' the street to bay me: every villain
Be call'd Posthumus Leonatus, and
Be villany less than 'twas! O Imogen!
My queen, my life, my wife! O Imogen,
Imogen, Imogen!

Imo. Peace, my lord; hear, hear—

Post. Shall 's have a play of this? Thou scornful page,
There lie thy part. [*Striking her: she falls.*

Pis. O, gentlemen, help!
Mine and your mistress! O, my lord Posthumus!
You ne'er kill'd Imogen till now. Help, help!
Mine honour'd lady!

Cym. Does the world go round?

Post. How came these staggers on me?

Pis. Wake, my mistress!

Cym. If this be so, the gods do mean to strike me
To death with mortal joy.

Pis. How fares my mistress?

Imo. O, get thee from my sight;
Thou gavest me poison: dangerous fellow, hence!
Breathe not where princes are.

Cym. The tune of Imogen!

Pis. Lady.
The gods throw stones of sulphur on me, if
That box I gave you was not thought by me
A precious thing: I had it from the queen.

Cym. New matter still?

Imo. It poison'd me.

Cor. O gods!

221 she herself, i. e., virtue herself.

223 bay: bark at.

225 villany less than 'twas: the word "villany" less abhorrent than it was.

227 hear, hear: (1) hear me, hear me; (2) Posthumus 误认为戏院里的喝彩声。

228 Shall's have: shall we make.

229 part: role.

230 Mine: my.

233 staggers: dizziness.

238 tune: voice.

240 stones of sulphur: thunderbolts.

I left out one thing which the queen confess'd,
Which must approve thee honest: 'If Pisanio
Have,' said she, 'given his mistress that confection
Which I gave him for cordial, she is served
As I would serve a rat.'

Cym. What 's this, Cornelius?

Cor. The queen, sir, very oft importuned me
To temper poisons for her, still pretending
The satisfaction of her knowledge only
In killing creatures vile, as cats and dogs,
Of no esteem: I, dreading that her purpose
Was of more danger, did compound for her
A certain stuff, which being ta'en would cease
The present power of life, but in short time
All offices of nature should again
Do their due functions. Have you ta'en of it?

Imo. Most like I did, for I was dead.

Bel. My boys,
There was our error.

Gui. This is, sure, Fidele.

Imo. Why did you throw your wedded lady from you?
Think that you are upon a rock, and now
Throw me again. [*Embracing him.*

Post. Hang there like fruit, my soul,
Till the tree die!

Cym. How now, my flesh, my child!
What, makest thou me a dullard in this act?
Wilt thou not speak to me?

Imo. [*Kneeling*] Your blessing, sir.

Bel. [*To Gui. and Arv.*] Though you did love this youth, I blame ye not;
You had a motive for 't.

Cym. My tears that fall
Prove holy water on thee! Imogen,

245 **approve**: prove.

246 **confection**: compound.

250 **temper**: mix. **still**: always.

252 **creatures vile**: creatures that were vile.

253 **esteem**: value.

254 **more**: greater.

255 **cease** (v. t.): halt.

257 **offices of nature**: natural faculties.

259 **like**: likely.

262 **rock**: cliff.

265 **dullard**: sluggish performer. **act**: play, drama.

268 **motive**: cause, reason.

Thy mother 's dead.
Imo. I am sorry for 't, my lord.
Cym. O, she was naught; and long of her it was
That we meet here so strangely: but her son
Is gone, we know not how nor where.
Pis. My lord,
Now fear is from me, I 'll speak troth. Lord Cloten,
Upon my lady's missing, came to me
With his sword drawn; foam'd at the mouth, and swore,
If I discovered not which way she was gone,
It was my instant death. By accident,
I had a feigned letter of my master's
Then in my pocket; which directed him
To seek her on the mountains near to Milford;
Where, in a frenzy, in my master's garments,
Which he enforced from me, away he posts
With unchaste purpose, and with oath to violate
My lady's honour: what became of him
I further know not.
Gui. Let me end the story:
I slew him there.
Cym. Marry, the gods forfend!
I would not thy good deeds should from my lips
Pluck a hard sentence: prithee, valiant youth,
Deny 't again.
Gui. I have spoke it, and I did it.
Cym. He was a prince.
Gui. A most incivil one: the wrongs he did me
Were nothing prince-like; for he did provoke me
With language that would make me spurn the sea,
If it could so roar to me: I cut off 's head;
And am right glad he is not standing here
To tell this tale of mine.

271 naught: wicked.

271 long of: along of, because of, owing to.

274 troth: truth.

277 discovered: revealed.

278 accident: coincidence.

279 feigned: dissembled (to mislead Imogen).

280 directed: led.

283 enforced: got by force (compulsion). **posts**: hastens.

287 Marry: by the Virgin Mary, a mild oath. **forfend**: forbid.

288 thy good deeds, i. e., you who have done good deeds (in the battle).

289 Deny 't again: take it back; 这个 again 是 back 之意。

290 spoke: spoken.

297 tell this tale of me: say that he cut off my head.

Cym. I am sorry for thee:
By thine own tongue thou art condemn'd, and must
Endure our law: thou 'rt dead.
Imo. That headless man
I thought had been my lord.
Cym. Bind the offender,
And take him from our presence.
Bel. Stay, sir king:
This man is better than the man he slew,
As well descended as thyself, and hath
More of thee merited than a band of Clotens
Had ever scar for. [*To the Guard*] Let his arms alone;
They were not born for bondage.
Cym. Why, old soldier,
Wilt thou undo the worth thou art unpaid for,
By tasting of our wrath? How of descent
As good as we?
Arv. In that he spake too far.
Cym. And thou shalt die for 't.
Bel. We will die all three
But I will prove that two on 's are as good
As I have given out him. My sons, I must
For mine own part unfold a dangerous speech,
Though haply well for you.
Arv. Your danger 's ours.
Gui. And our good his.
Bel. Have at it then, by leave.
Thou hadst, great king, a subject who
Was call'd Belarius.
Cym. What of him? He is
A banish'd traitor.
Bel. He it is that hath
Assumed this age, indeed a banish'd man;
I know not how a traitor.

304 **of thee merited**: deserved to get from you.

305 **Had ever scar for**: ever merited for their battle wounds. **Let his arms alone**: free his arms.

307 **undo**: ruin, annul. **worth**: merit. **unpaid**: not yet rewarded.

311 **But I will**: if I do not, unless I. **on 's**: of us.

312 **given out him**: declare him to be.

313 **For mine own part**: for myself,此短语修饰 dangerous.

314 **haply**: perhaps.

315 **Have at it**: listen, here it goes. **by leave**: with your permission.

319 **Assumed**: reached.

Cym. Take him hence:
The whole world shall not save him.
Bel. Not too hot:
First pay me for the nursing of thy sons;
And let it be confiscate all, so soon
As I have received it.
Cym. Nursing of my sons!
Bel. I am too blunt and saucy: here 's my knee:
Ere I arise I will prefer my sons;
Then spare not the old father. Mighty sir,
These two young gentlemen, that call me father
And think they are my sons, are none of mine;
They are the issue of your loins, my liege,
And blood of your begetting.
Cym. How! my issue!
Bel. So sure as you your father's. I, old Morgan,
Am that Belarius whom you sometime banish'd:
Your pleasure was my mere offence, my punishment
Itself, and all my treason: that I suffer'd
Was all the harm I did. These gentle princes—
For such and so they are—these twenty years
Have I train'd up: those arts they have as I
Could put into them; my breeding was, sir, as
Your highness knows. Their nurse, Euriphile,
Whom for the theft I wedded, stole these children
Upon my banishment: I moved her to 't,
Having received the punishment before
For that which I did then: beaten for loyalty
Excited me to treason: their dear loss,
The more of you 'twas felt, the more it shaped
Unto my end of stealing them. But, gracious sir,
Here are your sons again; and I must lose
Two of the sweet'st companions in the world.
The benediction of these covering heavens

321 **hot**：eager，anxious.

323 **it**，i. e.，the payment. **confiscate**：confiscated.

325 **saucy**：insolent.

326 **prefer**：advance，recommend for promotion.

330 **issue**：offspring. **loins**：腰部，生殖器。

333 **sometime**：once.

334 **Your pleasure … offence**：what you pleased (to accuse me of) was my entire offence.

338 **those**：such. **arts**：accomplishments.

342 **moved**：persuaded.

344 **beaten**：having been beaten.

345 **dear**：grievous.

346 **of**：by. **shaped**：suited，fitted.

347 **Unto**：with. **end**：purpose.

350 **The benediction**：may the blessing. **covering heavens**：旧时认为地的上空包着多层同心球层 spheres 或 spherical shells，或 orbs，上缀星座。

Fall on their heads like dew! For they are worthy
To inlay heaven with stars.

Cym. Thou weep'st, and speak'st.
The service that you three have done is more
Unlike than this thou tell'st. I lost my children:
If these be they, I know not how to wish
A pair of worthier sons.

Bel. Be pleased awhile.
This gentleman, whom I call Polydore,
Most worthy prince, as yours, is true Guiderius:
This gentleman, my Cadwal, Arviragus,
Your younger princely son; he, sir, was lapp'd
In a most curious mantle, wrought by the hand
Of his queen mother, which for more probation
I can with ease produce.

Cym. Guiderius had
Upon his neck a mole, a sanguine, star;
It is a mark of wonder.

Bel. This is he;
Who hath upon him still that natural stamp:
It was wise nature's end in the donation,
To be his evidence now.

Cym. O, what am I?
A mother to the birth of three? Ne'er mother
Rejoiced deliverance more. Blest pray you be,
That, after this strange starting from your orbs,
You may reign in them now! O Imogen,
Thou hast lost by this a kingdom.

Imo. No, my lord;
I have got two worlds by 't. O my gentle brothers,
Have we thus met? O, never say hereafter
But I am truest speaker: you call'd me brother,
When I was but your sister; I you brothers,
When ye were so indeed.

352 inlay heaven with stars：become constellations. 传说最优秀的人死后变成星座。

354 Unlike：improbable，incredible.

355 wish：wish to have，desire.

360 lapp'd：wrapped.

361 curious：exquisitely made.

362 probation：proof.

364 sanguine：blood-red.

365 of wonder：wonderful.

367 end：purpose. **donation**：giving.

369—70 Never deliverance（giving birth）rejoiced mother more；倒装。

370 you,指两个儿子,以及主宰他们的两颗星辰。

371 strange starting from your orbs：unnatural shooting from your spheres.

372 them，i. e.，your orbs. 旧时认为天体离开其轨道为反常,恢复到原轨道才是正常。

373 lost a kingdom,两个哥哥回来,小妹不再能继承王位。

Cym. Did you e'er meet?
Arv. Ay, my good lord.
Gui. And at first meeting loved,
Continued so, until we thought he died.
Cor. By the queen's dram she swallow'd.
Cym. O rare instinct!
When shall I hear all through? This fierce abridgement
Hath to it circumstantial branches, which
Distinction should be rich in. Where? How lived you?
And when came you to serve our Roman captive?
How parted with your brothers? How first met them?
Why fled you from the court? And whither? These,
And your three motives to the battle, with
I know not how much more, should be demanded;
And all the other by-dependances,
From chance to chance: but nor the time nor place
Will serve our long inter'gatories. See,
Posthumus anchors upon Imogen;
And she, like harmless lightning, throws her eye
On him, her brothers, me, her master, hitting
Each object with a joy: the counterchange
Is severally in all. Let 's quit this ground,
And smoke the temple with our sacrifices.
[*To Belarius*] Thou art my brother; so we 'll hold thee ever.
Imo. You are my father too; and did relieve me,
To see this gracious season.
Cym. All o'erjoy'd,
Save these in bonds: let them be joyful too,
For they shall taste our comfort.
Imo. My good master,
I will yet do you service.
Luc. Happy be you!
Cym. The forlorn soldier that so nobly fought,

381 dram: pernicious potion,小量毒酒。 **instinct**：指前述兄妹相亲的本能。

382 fierce abridgement: drastically compressed account.

383 branches: ramifications.

384 Distinction should be rich in: should be abundant when being distinguished.

388 your three motives: the motives of you three.

390 by-dependances: circumstances hanging from these.

391 chance: event. **nor … nor**: neither … nor.

392 inter'gatories: questioning.

393 anchors upon, i. e., clings to.

396 counterchange: interchange, exchange (of glances).

397 severally in all: from each to each.

398 smoke: fill with smoke. 祭品是烧掉的,故生烟。

400 relieve: free from distress.

401 gracious: happy.

403 comfort: happiness.

405 forlorn: lost, missing.

He would have well becomed this place and graced
The thankings of a king.
Post. I am, sir,
The soldier that did company these three
In poor beseeming; 'twas a fitment for
The purpose I then follow'd. That I was he,
Speak, Iachimo: I had you down, and might
Have made you finish.
Iach. [*Kneeling*] I am down again:
But now my heavy conscience sinks my knee,
As then your force did. Take that life, beseech you,
Which I so often owe: but your ring first;
And here the bracelet of the truest princess
That ever swore her faith.
Post. Kneel not to me:
The power that I have on you is to spare you;
The malice towards you to forgive you: live,
And deal with others better.
Cym. Nobly doom'd!
We 'll learn our freeness of a son-in-law;
Pardon 's the word to all.
Arv. [*To Posthumus*] You holp us, sir,
As you did mean indeed to be our brother;
Joy'd are we that you are.
Post. Your servant, princes. Good my lord of Rome,
Call forth your soothsayer: as I slept, methought
Great Jupiter, upon his eagle back'd,
Appear'd to me, with other spritely shows
Of mine own kindred: when I waked, I found
This label on my bosom; whose containing
Is so from sense in hardness, that I can
Make no collection of it: let him show
His skill in the construction.
Luc. Philarmonus!

406 **becomed**：honoured. **graced**：adorned，dignified.
408 **company** (v. t.)：be the companion of.
409 **beseeming**：appearance. **fitment**：suitable disguise.
412 **finish**：die.
415 **often**：many times over.
420 **doom'd**：judged，sentenced.
421 **freeness**：generosity，nobility.
422 **holp**：helped.
423 **As**：as if.
427 **back'd**：mounted.
428 **spritely**：having the quality of a spirit，ghostly.
429 **waked**：woke up.
430 **label**：tablet. **containing**：content.
431 **from sense in hardness**：hard to make sense of.
432 **collection**：inference，conclusion.
433 **construction**：construing，interpretation.

Sooth. Here, my good lord.

Luc. Read, and declare the meaning.

Sooth. [*Reads*] 'When as a lion's whelp shall, to himself unknown, without seeking find, and be embraced by a piece of tender air, and when from a stately cedar shall be lopped branches, which, being dead many years, shall after revive, be jointed to the old stock and freshly grow, then shall Posthumus end his miseries, Britain be fortunate and flourish in peace and plenty.'
Thou, Leonatus, art the lion's whelp;
The fit and apt construction of thy name,
Being Leo-natus, doth import so much.
[*To Cymbeline*] The piece of tender air, thy virtuous daughter,
Which we call 'mollis aer'; and 'mollis aer'
We term it 'mulier': which 'mulier' I divine
Is this most constant wife; who even now,
Answering the letter of the oracle,
Unknown to you, unsought, were clipp'd about
With this most tender air.

Cym. This hath some seeming.

Sooth. The lofty cedar, royal Cymbeline,
Personates thee: and thy lopp'd branches point
Thy two sons forth; who, by Belarius stol'n,
For many years thought dead, are now revived,
To the most majestic cedar join'd, whose issue
Promises Britain peace and plenty.

Cym. Well;
My peace we will begin. And, Caius Lucius,
Although the victor, we submit to Cæsar
And to the Roman empire, promising
To pay our wonted tribute, from the which
We were dissuaded by our wicked queen;

435—442 见 V. iv. 138—145.

447 mollis aer [拉丁]: gentle air.

448 mulier [拉丁]: woman. 认为 mollis aer 是 mulier 的字源,乃是俗传的错误。

450 answering: agreeing with. **letter**: terms.

451 were 前省略 you. **clipp'd about**: embraced.

452 seeming: appearance of being, likelihood.

454 personates: stands for.

Whom heavens in justice both on her and hers
Have laid most heavy hand.

Sooth. The fingers of the powers above do tune
The harmony of this peace. The vision,
Which I made known to Lucius ere the stroke
Of this yet scarce-old battle, at this instant
Is full accomplish'd; for the Roman eagle,
From south to west on wing soaring aloft,
Lessen'd herself and in the beams o' the sun
So vanish'd: which foreshow'd our princely eagle,
The imperial Cæsar, should again unite
His favour with the radiant Cymbeline,
Which shines here in the west.

Cym. Laud we the gods;
And let our crooked smokes climb to their nostrils
From our blest altars. Publish we this peace
To all our subjects. Set we forward: let
A Roman and a British ensign wave
Friendly together: so through Lud's town march;
And in the temple of great Jupiter
Our peace we 'll ratify; seal it with feasts.
Set on there! Never was a war did cease,
Ere bloody hands were wash'd, with such a peace.

[*Exeunt.*

464 **Whom**: on whom. **hers**, i. e., Cloten.

469 **yet scarce-cold**: yet scarcely finished,复合形容词。

470 **full**: fully, entirely.

476 **Laud we**: let us praise.

477 **crooked**: curling.

478 **Publish we**: let us proclaim.

479 **Set we forward**: let us go forward.

480 **ensign**: banner.

484 **Set on there**: March forth. **did cease**: that ceased.

图书在版编目(CIP)数据

辛白林/(英)莎士比亚(Shakespeare, W.)著;裘克安注释. —北京:商务印书馆,2007
(莎士比亚注释丛书)
ISBN 7-100-04972-5

I. 辛… II. ①莎… ②裘… III. ①英语—语言读物②传奇剧(话剧)—剧本—英国—中世纪 IV. H319.4:I

中国版本图书馆CIP数据核字(2006)第031968号

莎士比亚注释丛书

XĪNBÁILÍN

辛 白 林

裘克安 注释

商 务 印 书 馆 出 版
(北京王府井大街36号 邮政编码 100710)
商 务 印 书 馆 发 行
北 京 瑞 古 冠 中 印 刷 厂 印 刷
ISBN 7-100-04972-5/H·1222

2007年12月第1版 开本787×960 1/32
2007年12月北京第1次印刷 印张8¼ 插页1

定价:14.00元